Building Partnerships

A Realtor's Step-by-Step Guide to New Home Sales Success

Robert E. Hafer, MIRM, CSP, GSP

Copyright © 2026 by Robert E. Hafer

Printed in the United States of America
Published by REH Publishing
Edited by Douglas R. Hafer, Partner at Currnutt and Hafer, L.L.P.
Cover Design by 100 Covers
Foreword by Charlie Roter, Vice President of Sales, Empire Homes

Dedication

*T*o My Grandchildren,

I dedicate this book to my grandchildren and great-grandchildren. You have given me so much pleasure and love. You are always in my thoughts and prayers for now and forevermore.

About Bob Hafer

DURING BOB HAFER'S FIRST 23 years in the home building industry, he held numerous positions with a national home builder, ranging from on-site salesperson to management in marketing, merchandising, research, and product development, and as a divisional and regional president.

Then, for 15 years, he provided sales training and marketing expertise to over 100 home builders nationwide. During that time, he was featured as a subject matter expert in nationally recognized media, including Builder Magazine, Builder Radio, Realtor, Realty Times, The Real Estate Professional, Texas Builder, Texas Homebuilder, and Professional Builder.

To complement his new home experience, he earned a Texas Real Estate License in 2009. He has experienced everything a Realtor is responsible for, including lead generation, sales, marketing, administration, contract and client management. He quickly learned that being a Realtor was far more complex and demanding than selling homes for a builder.

In 2010, he became the Director of Builder Sales for the largest real estate broker in Dallas, Ebby Halliday Realtors. In that position, he was responsible for developing working relationships between Dallas builders and Ebby's family of real estate associates and increasing company revenue through builder sales and listings.

He was awarded the Professional Realtor of the Year in 2011 and 2012 for Outstanding Service to the Dallas Builders Association (DBA). During that time, he also served on the DBA's Board of Directors, chaired their Ambassadors Committee, and served on the Professional Development and Curriculum Committee for the MetroTex Association of Realtors.

As a DBA Board of Directors member, he was asked to investigate the possibility of developing a training program to bridge the knowledge gap between builders and Realtors. He presented the idea to the Dallas MetroTex Association of Realtors and received an overwhelmingly positive response. So, in 2013, he developed a six-seminar builder series entitled *Have You Considered New*. The class was awarded the *"Marketing Program of the Year"* by the Texas Realtors Association.

In 2014, he joined HomesUSA.com, where he was responsible for developing new businesses with builders in Dallas, San Antonio, Austin, and Houston. HomesUSA manages builder MLS listings, provides marketing support, and assists builders in identifying Realtors who desire to sell new homes.

In 2016, he co-founded alongside Ben Caballero HomesUSAAlliance.com. The Alliance aimed to connect builders and Realtors through education and communication.

In 2023, he left HomesUSA.com and HomesUSAAlliance.com and began outlining a series of books he wanted to write to teach Realtors how to work and connect with the new home builder community. The books will be based on the seven continuing education classes he developed.

Content will range from building partnerships with local and national volume home builders to introducing the possibility of new homes to their clients, to understanding the new home construction process, to an appreciation for the value of the green building process, to best practices for negotiating with new home builders, and finally, how to read a new home construction blueprint. It is an ambitious undertaking that will take many years to complete, but one he feels compelled to write.

Over the years, he maintained his Texas Real Estate license while teaching thousands of Realtors how to sell new homes. During that time, he has never forgotten how challenging a Realtor's job is. He learned through personal experiences that being a Realtor is hard work. It is demanding mentally, physically, and financially, and most importantly, a Realtor does not manage their own time; time manages them.

Foreword

My name is Charlie Roter, I am the Vice President of Sales for Empire Homes in Colorado Springs, CO. I have worked in the new home industry for over thirty-five years, and I have been a licensed broker since 2004 in California and now Colorado, working in various roles from Sales Consultant, National Sales Coach, to Vice President of Sales and Marketing.

Bob Hafer has been a mentor, coach and friend to me throughout my career. I was extremely excited to read this book. The home building industry has always established partnerships with Realtors and brokers, as they are a tremendous resource for prospective buyers. Most new home builders average 60% to 70% of their annual sales through referrals from Realtors. These relationships are critical to a home builder's success.

Throughout my career in the new home industry, I have met Realtors who have become new home specialists. I have often wondered why more Realtors do not consider this option and strictly rely only on resale listings. Selling new homes is an excellent opportunity for a long and lucrative career as a Realtor. As Bob so superbly details in this book, you will need to invest time and effort; however, this book will outline precisely what you need to do and accomplish. In this book, Bob lays out an incredible roadmap to attaining success as a Realtor. Are you willing and open to exploring the new home construction process?

Building Partnerships: A Realtor's Step-by-Step Guide to New Home Sales Success is the most complete book on how to understand and navigate your way through the new home building process. Developing relationships with reputable and quality builders can be the vehicle to a long and successful career as a Realtor. Bob addresses the most asked questions from Realtors regarding the new home process.

- Can I trust new home builders?

- Will they try to leave me out of the process?

- Will they communicate with us?

- What if they do not deliver a quality experience and a home for my clients?

- How does a Realtor referral commission work for me?

Bob explains the critical components in each step of the new home process, from choosing the right builder for you and your clients, design and option selections, the value of establishing a relationship with new home sales consultants, to negotiating and finding the absolute best home for your client.

Having successfully worked in both the new home industry and as a licensed Realtor for years, Bob is uniquely qualified to be an authority on new home builders, explaining the sales and construction process in a clear and understandable manner.

In a ubiquitous world of new home builders, *Building Partnerships: A Realtor's Step-by-Step Guide to New Home Sales Success* delivers extreme clarity to Realtors who desire to add an intriguing and rewarding layer to their business. Bob motivates you to go beyond the usual new home model visit and inspires you to take it to another level. To serve your clients as true professionals, and helping you become your best self as a Realtor.

Building Partnerships: A Realtor's Step-by-Step Guide to New Home Sales Success is a rare and inspiring book that comes at the right time.

Introduction

CONGRATULATIONS ON MAKING NEW home sales part of your real estate business strategy. When you purchased this book, you opened up the possibility of increasing your sales and income for years to come. But buying the book will not be enough to guarantee your success. What you do with the strategies I share throughout this book will be what advances your real estate career. However, none of my home builder approaches will work until you do one critical thing: start.

Allow me to recount a personal anecdote about starting. As the Director of Builder Sales for a prominent Dallas real estate company, I provided new home sales training to over 1600 agents. During a two-hour CE-approved seminar on working with the new home builder community, I referenced five books to reinforce a teaching point. At the break, an agent approached me, questioning if I had read all those books. I handed him a text and asked him to open it. He found highlighted passages and scribbled notes in the margins. He then asked, *"How did you do it?"* My response was straightforward, *"I started."*

After the break and before the seminar resumed, he raised his hand and asked if he could address the other agents. I nodded my agreement. He proceeded to share the conversation we had during the break. He talked about the books and how they were marked up. He then spoke about his question and my answer. He said, "*I have been a real estate agent for fifteen years. I have attended hundreds of hours of continuing education training and learned a lot, but today, I discovered it doesn't matter what I want to accomplish; it will not happen unless I start. It's really that simple. Start, and I have taken the first step to whatever I want to accomplish.*"

Life Gets In the Way

You might ask, "*Why tell this story?*" You might think, "*I start, what is the big deal?*" Well, my experience is that most agents I have taught are procrastinators, not because it is what they want, but because life gets in the way. Things they are asked to do get put on hold because a child needs to be picked up from school or dropped off for practice. A birthday celebration needs attention, a memorable vacation needs planning, and holidays happen.

Life consists of things that require your attention. Each is important; those things wouldn't be the same without your involvement. But remember, prioritizing and overcoming procrastination is not just a strategy; it's a mindset crucial to your success in new home sales. It will keep you inspired and driven to achieve your sales goals.

I understand you have a busy life, but if you genuinely want to benefit from what I am about to share, you must make some adjustments. It's crucial to prioritize the tasks you will be asked to do. This includes thinking, reading, writing, completing to-do lists, researching builders and the products they offer, meeting with a builder's on-site agent and construction manager, decorators, mortgage specialists, title companies, updating social media, and, most importantly, networking your new home knowledge with your family, friends, and acquaintances. Remember, none of this will happen unless you plan for it and start.

To maintain a real estate license, you make a financial investment in yourself. Don't let that money go to waste. This is your opportunity to take control of your future. My goal is to help you succeed in new home sales. Your goal is to put in the work necessary to succeed.

Building Partnerships

Because you are an independent contractor, you probably have no one to turn to for help. Adding new home sales to your business strategy will eliminate many administrative tasks you are responsible for in existing home sales, and transfer those obligations to a builders' staff. In other words, selling new homes will make your job, as a real estate agent, easier.

Builders want to partner with you; my advice is, let them. When you partner with a builder, you will be the agent they seek to list and sell their inventory homes. You will be the agent that the on-site salesperson contacts when a client wants to purchase a new home but has a house to sell and is not represented. You will be the agent your clients refer to friends, relatives, and acquaintances because you provided excellent advice throughout the new home sales, mortgage, construction, closing, and service process.

This book, *Building Partnerships: A Realtor's Step-by-Step Guide to New Home Sales Success*, outlines in great detail everything you require to build those partnerships. Take time with each chapter; don't rush from one chapter to another. If you don't understand something I have written, reread the chapter until you comprehend it. In some chapters, you will be asked to perform tasks. When you complete a task, you have learned something that will demonstrate your difference to a builder and, more importantly, will set you up for success with future home buyers. And finally, at the end of each chapter, there are three questions. Please take the time to answer those questions. The benefit is that you are creating your roadmap to new home sales success.

Working with and training thousands of new home salespeople and Realtors taught me that agents willing to do what their peers are unwilling to do are unique in the real estate industry. Embrace that uniqueness; don't follow the easy road. Let this book and the books to follow guide you through the steps you must take while providing all the knowledge you need to make your effort pay dividends in additional sales, income, and job security for years to come.

So, are you ready to build your real estate business through new home sales? If the answer is "*Yes*," then let's get started.

Table of Contents

Multi-Family Home Builders

YOU HAVE FOUR NEW home builder partner possibilities. They are multi-family, custom, semi-custom, and volume home builders. As you will see, each builder partner has positives and negatives. After researching, you can choose the builder type you want to partner with. However, you need to be cautious about who you choose because the builder you pick will be seen as a referral when you introduce them to your client. I am sure you agree that your success in new or resale properties mainly depends of the referrals you receive or give.

So, as you choose, I hope you consider this: a strong working relationship between you and the builder is necessary. If you feel uncomfortable with a builder or the builder's on-site representative, please trust your instincts and move on. Remember this thought as you select your builder partners: builders are like buses; miss one, wait a few minutes, and another builder will appear. And, like the story of the Three Bears, the next builder may be *"Just right."*

So, let's begin your journey in finding a builder partner that is *"Just right"* for you and your future new home buyer clients by taking an in-depth look at multi-family builders.

Various Types of Multifamily Dwellings

The following are the various types of multifamily dwellings and the characteristics that distinguish them. As you will see, there are numerous types of multifamily options. Each dwelling type will attract a different buyer. Therefore, at least part of your consideration for including multi-family builders in your new home sales business plan should be based on the buyers you work with, where you live, and whether multi-family housing is available for sale or lease in your market area.

Apartments

Apartments are one of the most common types of multifamily dwellings. Apartment buildings are typically owned by a single entity, such as a real estate investment trust (REIT) or a property management company. Individual apartment units are rented out, not sold. Apartments often feature common areas and amenities, including swimming pools, gyms, and play areas. Maintenance, property decisions, and management responsibilities fall onto the property owner, not the renter.

Duplex

A duplex is a multifamily dwelling comprising two separate living units within a single building. The two units typically mirror each other in layout and size, with shared walls. Each unit has its own entrance, generally located on opposite sides of the dwelling, which provides its occupants with privacy. Duplexes can be owned or rented, with the maintenance and upkeep typically falling to the property owner.

Townhouse

A townhouse is a multifamily dwelling characterized by a multi-level design and units that share walls on one or two sides. Townhouses are often arranged in rows or clusters to create a community-style appearance. Each townhome has its own entrance and may feature a small private patio, shared common areas, and access to a pool and other recreational amenities. Townhouses may be rented or bought, and common spaces are maintained through a homeowners' association (HOA).

Condominiums

Condominiums refer to a group of individually owned units. Condominiums can be detached units, similar to villas, or they may have two or more units within a single building. Regardless of the structure type, each unit in a condominium building is owned by an individual who holds the deed to that unit. Condo owners pay fees to maintain and share common areas and amenities, including swimming pools, gym and fitness centers, parking structures, landscaping, and outdoor spaces. Condo owners own the interior of their homes but may have shared ownership of shared walls and common areas. Maintenance for shared areas is typically the responsibility of the Homeowners Association (HOA).

Aged-Restricted Housing

Age-restricted housing is designed for individuals of a specific age group, typically 55 years and older. These communities often offer amenities and services specifically designed for older adults, including recreational facilities and social activities. Various dwellings, such as apartments or condos, can be featured in an age-restricted community. An HOA or similar organization usually maintains the shared areas and is supported by monthly dues.

Mixed Use Properties

Mixed-use properties combine residential and commercial spaces. These properties often feature apartments or condos on the upper floors and commercial spaces, such as retail stores or offices, on the ground floor. Mixed-use properties foster communities by combining residential spaces with carefully designed commercial areas. While mixed-use properties are often owned by a REIT or a property management company, the residential units within them may be bought or rented. This type of dwelling is common in high-density urban settings.

GATHERING INFORMATION

From the descriptions above, numerous multi-family opportunities exist to earn income through lease or sales commissions. Let's suppose the idea of partnering with a multi-family builder interests you. In that case, you must gather information to understand what type of multi-family housing is right for you and your clients. I am sure you use the Internet to answer your clients' real estate questions; therefore, why not use it to gather information about multi-family builders in your market area?

To begin, consider the following three steps. First, type multi-family builders into your favorite search engine. You will see page after page of references to different multi-family builders. Take your time collecting information because not all multi-family builders are the same, and those differences distinguish one from another.

Second, suppose your brokerage sales meetings are anything like the ones I have attended. In that case, you have the opportunity to discuss other agents' issues or questions you may have. Please take this opportunity to inform them that you wish to incorporate multi-family new home sales and leasing into your business plan and require their assistance. Ask them to contact you to discuss any multi-family builders they have worked with. Tell them not to hold back on any information, good or bad, because you know that recommending a multi-family property or builder to a buyer is a referral.

Thirdly, contact your local Home Builders Association (HBA) and inquire about the builders within the Association who specialize in multi-family construction. Request a comprehensive list of those builders, including their contact details.

While speaking to the HBA representative, inquire about membership costs. The HBA offers different types of membership, including builder members, associate members, and affiliate members. The price varies by membership level, with builder members being the most expensive and affiliate members being the least expensive. I suggest this because you may want to make membership in the Association a part of your business plan. By becoming a member, you can attend all builder meetings and events. As a member, you will get to know the builders as individuals — someone interested in their success and willing to refer them to their clients.

By following these recommendations, you will have compiled an impressive list of multi-family builders. Now, the real work begins. Please visit each builder's website for more specific information. Yes, this exercise will take time, but it is well spent if you want multi-family sales and leases to be part of your new home business plan.

I know I maybe asking you to do things you have never done before, but you never know what future clients might want. Remember, your clients are motivated by different things: some want to rent, others want to own, while others seek to downsize, and some prefer an urban lifestyle, others a suburban one, and others want to invest. You never know what a client wants; you must be prepared to satisfy every need.

COMPENSATION

A couple of key points to note about compensation are that you are the only person interested in your compensation, and it is negotiable. Stop, don't read any further. Now, reread what you just read. It is vitally important that you understand what I have written because it is true. For this reason, it is advantageous for you and your multi-family builder of choice to agree on how you will be compensated. Don't assume you will earn three percent on leases and sales alike. In today's market, commissions are negotiable. The knowledge you gain by gathering multi-family information will help you understand what commissions builders pay for sales and leases. The following is critical: any commission arrangement must be in writing and be part of the sales or lease agreement.

Don't be afraid to discuss compensation with the builder or leasing company. Your time, talent, and expertise are to be rewarded. People are willing to pay for professionalism. Just ensure that you are worth the compensation you receive.

BUILDING PARTNERSHIPS

Before moving on to Chapter Two, please take a few minutes to answer some questions about what you have just read. The questions are meant to support your understanding of the material covered in each chapter. I recommend writing your answers in the space provided between questions or in a notebook that will include your key takeaways form each chapter. I promise your answers will serve as a helpful future guide as you develop new partnerships throughout the new home builder community.

CHAPTER ONE KEY TAKEAWAYS

Chapter One provides an overview of the key aspects you need to know when thinking about partnering with a multi-family home builder. To reinforce your understanding of the material in this chapter, take a few minutes to answer the following three questions? Answering these key takeaways will strengthen your understanding of the chapter's main ideas and aid your ongoing learning about working and partnering with the new home builder community.

1. What spoke to you most about this chapter?

2. What insight in these pages made the most significant impression on you?

3. How will you take what you have learned in this chapter, and put it into action in your pursuit of new home sales?

Custom Home Builders

WHEN CLIENTS BEGIN A new home search, they will likely encounter the term custom frequently. The term is vague, as home builders employ it in various contexts. For some builders, a custom-built home means that your client can choose some interior and exterior finishes, but the floor plan is mostly predetermined. In my opinion, that describes a semi-custom or volume builder home versus a custom home.

When a true custom home is built, your client controls the end product completely. Your client meets with a home designer to discuss their housing needs in-depth, creating a customized plan that meets their specific requirements. All options are at their disposal, and they alone are the final arbitrator. The result is a unique home that perfectly fits their family's personality.

Does a Custom Home Always Start from a Blank Page?

As stated before, your client is the final arbitrator of a custom-built home. They may know exactly how they want their home laid out and the precise measurements of each room. If your client can fully describe what they want, the builder's design group should be able to develop a blueprint that reflects their vision. But, as you will learn, some clients are anxious about starting with a blank page. Many clients want to start with floor plan examples that they can modify and refine. After seeing a visual representation, they can rearrange bedrooms, enlarge kitchens, add custom rooms, and more. The final floor plan may not resemble their starting point; it is a custom build, but the initial floor plan helped your client reach their destination.

Custom Home Limitations

Unlike volume and semi-custom homes, custom builds have only budget and space limitations to consider. Your client decides on every aspect of the build, from flooring to layout, cabinets and countertops, lighting fixtures, etc. They can change the smallest detail, like USB options in their electrical outlets. Just remember to lean on the builder's expertise to keep your client's design and construction ideas practical and on budget.

Custom Home Building Timeline

Prepare your client for a timeline that may reach two years from start to finish. Below is a rough breakdown you can share with your client of each step in the process of completion of a custom home and an estimate of the time each element may take:

Pre-construction: 9 – 12 months

- Assemble the team (architect/home designer, builder, and bids) – 3 months

- Secure a homesite – 2 months

- Design (style, floor plan, options, selections) – 3 to 6 months

- Permits and loan approval – 1 month

Construction: 12 Months

- Documents (plans, specs, bids, and contracts) – 2 months

- Site prep (clear, grade, level, and stake) – 1 month

- Foundation (pour footings, foundation, basement, slab; install drain tile) – 1 1/2 months

- Rough carpentry (frame walls, floors, roof; install sheathing, house wrap) – 2 months

- Install HVAC – 1 month

- Rough plumbing, electrical, audio/visual, security – 2 ½ months

- Roofing, exterior siding/brick/trim, windows, doors – 1 ½ months

- Insulation and drywall – 1 ½ months

- Prime, caulk, paint – 3 months

- Flooring, cabinets, trim, hardware – 4 months

- Cleaning, punch list, closing – 1 month

Custom Home Variables

The timeline for a custom home can vary significantly due to many factors outside the builder's control. These variables include:

- The size and complexity of the home design.

- Securing permits can vary greatly depending on the city or county building department.

- Shortages of available supplies or subcontractors.

- Site conditions may also add to building time.

- Bad weather, including heavy rains, snow, or freezing temperatures, can cause significant construction delays.

- Design selections and changes during construction are a common and profound contributor to the time it takes to design and build a custom home.

The bottom line for you is to advise your clients to be prepared for delays, often outside a builder's control. Ask your client not to be the reason for a delay. Instruct them to select according to the builder's schedule and avoid making any changes during construction.

Finding a Custom Builder for You and Your Clients

Finding a custom home builder you are comfortable referring is a time-consuming process that requires thorough research. However, the rewards are worth your effort once you have found the right custom builder for you and your clients. Start your search by contacting your local HBA and explaining that you want to offer custom building services to your clients. Ask for a list of custom builders in your area. My advice is to select three builders from the list and begin doing your research.

What follows is the type of information you will need to narrow down your search for a suitable custom builder:

- **<u>Determine if the builder has a reputable business</u>**: A top-notch professional integrates best construction practices, writes clear contracts, maintains insurance, provides warranties, and offers an excellent after-closing service program.

- **<u>Ask about pricing and payment schedules</u>**: Before beginning the work, a qualified custom builder will provide a written estimate, a final budget, and a detailed contract.

- **<u>Ask about their custom home experience</u>**: A custom builder usually shares how long they have been in business. Longevity suggests financial stability, which is necessary to complete the job and still be available when problems arise after the job is finished. Also, the more homes the builder has completed, the more expertise they bring to your client's home.

- **<u>Always ask for references and contact them</u>**: Any high-quality custom builder should be willing to provide you with satisfied customers' names and phone numbers. If they cannot consider that a red flag and walk away.

When contacting former clients, ask about all the project pieces, which include:

1. How effectively did the builder adhere to the initial plans?

2. Did the builder meet and exceed expectations with the home's main features, build time, budget, and after-sale service?

3. Ask the most telling question: Would they hire the builder again if they had to do it all over?

I said this would take time, and it will. I can't say it enough: ***"When you introduce a builder to a client, that is a referral."*** As a Realtor, your success will be measured by referrals. When you do your research, you can confidently refer a builder. If asked, you can provide your client with your research findings. As you read this book, you will learn that your research enables clients to make an informed decision about a home builder. Your client will show their appreciation by referring you to family and friends.

Now, let's take a look at how custom builders compensate agents.

COMPENSATION

First, as mentioned earlier, you are the only person interested in your compensation. Secondly, your commission will most likely be negotiable, especially with custom home builders. For this reason, it is advantageous for you and your chosen builder to agree on how you will be compensated. Your commission will depend on whether you are acting as the seller's agent for the builder or as the buyer's agent for the buyer.

As the builder's seller's agent, your compensation will be negotiated with the builder. As a buyer's agent, your compensation will be negotiated with the buyer and included as a line item in the final budget for new home construction. In both instances, you, the builder, or you and your client will sign a written addendum to be included in the final contract.

When you choose a custom builder to partner with, ask how their to-be-built sales are mortgaged. You might be surprised to learn that most custom builders utilize a one-time construction loan, also known as a construction-to-permanent loan. This loan combines financing for the construction of a home and a permanent mortgage into a single loan and closing process, saving your client time and money. Additionally, a one-time construction loan benefits you because your commission is paid at the start of construction, rather than at closing.

Always discuss commission percentages with the builder or your buyer, and ensure that the agreed-upon terms are in writing and included in the contract. As mentioned earlier, your time, talent, and expertise must be rewarded. People are willing to pay for professionalism. Just make sure you are worth the commission you are receiving.

Your Compensation Percentage – It Depends

Your commission percentage depends on whether you act as the builder's or buyer's buying agent. You may encounter three scenarios when working with a custom home builder.

Scenario #1

Suppose you have listed a builder's inventory home. In this case, your role is to show value in the house's different features, refer questions to the builder, follow up with the prospective buyers to confirm questions were answered to the potential buyer's satisfaction, obtain a contract agreement complete with signatures, assist with mortgage approval, communicate with the title company about closing date and time, and lastly, stop by, after closing, to welcome them to the neighborhood, and ask for a testimonial and referral.

Scenario #2

Suppose you are the builder's buying and selling agent tasked with finding suitable lots to build on in an area of town that is transitioning from older homes built on large lots to custom-built homes. The builder's interest is in the size of the lot, not the existing house. The builder will demolish the older home and replace it with a custom build. In this situation, you act as the buyer's buying agent, purchasing the older home, and represent the builder as their selling agent for the newly built custom home.

Your role as the builder's buying agent includes research and negotiation. As the builder's selling agent, your role encompasses all the responsibilities outlined in Scenario #1. In these roles, you will earn two commissions. So, the rewards are excellent, but the time invested can be lengthy.

Scenario #3

In this scenario, you represent a client interested in building a custom home. Your role is to locate a custom builder who will meet your client's needs; it must be someone you and they can trust during the planning, budgeting, construction, and closing phases, and have a good reputation for handling issues that develop after closing. Once you and your client have decided on a suitable builder, you will assume the responsibilities outlined in Scenario #1 as a buyer's agent.

Your Role

As you can easily see, your role with a custom builder varies depending on the situation, and with these changes, your commission percentage also changes. You will wear many hats when you work with a custom builder. So, as Forrest Gump said, ***"Life is like a box of chocolates; you never know what you're going to get."*** If you work with the custom-built community, just be prepared for the unexpected. However, don't let that be why you move away from working with custom builders; the unexpected also comes with substantial commissions.

Chapter Two Key Takeaways

Chapter Two provides an overview of the key aspects you need to know when thinking about partnering with a custom home builder. To reinforce your understanding of the material in this chapter take a few minutes to answer the following three questions? Answering these key takeaways will strengthen your understanding of the chapter's main ideas and aid your ongoing learning about working and partnering with the new home builder community.

1.   What spoke to you most about this chapter?

2.   What insight in these pages made the most significant impression on you?

3.   How will you take what you have learned in this chapter, and put it into action in your pursuit of new home sales?

Semi-Custom Home Builders

SEMI-CUSTOM HOMES ARE THE "in-between" option, falling between a production home and a custom home. They are a perfect choice if your client wants to have a say in certain home features but doesn't want to have to make every single product decision.

With a semi-custom home, your client will choose between pre-designed floor plans that a builder has already developed. Once they have selected a plan, they can customize the design with the assistance of a staff home designer or an outside architect. Some changes include structural modifications, such as replacing windows, relocating interior walls, adding a room, or expanding garage space. The client typically gets to choose flooring, appliances, cabinetry, light fixtures, and materials such as brick, stone, and stucco.

The Pros and Cons of Semi-Custom Home Building

The benefits of building a semi-custom home include that it is completed faster, costs less than a custom home, reduces your client's decision-making, and offers fewer surprises during the construction process.

The cons are that building materials and finishes will be somewhat limited, the floor plan may not be fully customizable, and the construction process will not be under their control.

What are the Cost Differences Between Custom and Semi-Custom Home Building

As I have written, semi-custom homes offer pre-designed floor plans that can be customized to some degree, while still allowing clients to personalize their chosen home while staying within a budget. Additionally, semi-custom homes offer cost savings because builders can leverage their existing home designs and materials across multiple projects. This emphasis on cost savings can make potential homebuyers feel financially safe.

On the other hand, custom homes are built from the ground up, involving more personalization and attention to detail, which results in higher costs. This emphasis on personalization and attention to detail can make potential homebuyers feel the luxury and exclusivity of a custom home. Custom home costs can also increase based on design, size, materials, and site-specific conditions. For instance, if a client desires high-end architectural finishes or the lot they select has rugged terrain, these requirements can significantly impact the overall cost.

Whether your client is drawn to the flexibility and cost-effectiveness of a semi-custom design or is set on a fully customized home, it's crucial to consider design, personalization, site selection, and budget. Understanding these factors will empower them to make informed decisions that align with their vision and financial plan.

COMPENSATION

The commission you receive from a semi-custom builder will be similar to the compensation you receive from a volume home builder. In most situations, a semi-custom builder is part of a volume builder's overall business plan. The only difference is that the semi-custom undertaking is marketed differently.

An example of this is Highland Homes, a highly successful company based in Dallas, Texas. Highland Homes caters to entry-level home buyers under the HHS Residential Brand, move-up buyers under the Highland Homes brand, and semi-custom buyers under the Huntington Homes brand. These are three distinct companies, each targeting a different home buyer, but all owned and managed by the same company.

Your commission is included as a line item in the house budget. However, in most instances, your commission is budgeted between 2.25% and 2.5 0%. The percentage difference is based on comparing Realtor-assisted and non-Realtor-assisted sales that the builder experiences year-over-year. Most volume builders average between 60% to 70% of all sales, with the home buyer represented by a Realtor; therefore, volume builders only budget for your commission according to the expected percentage of Realtor sales.

Architectural Changes

The most significant difference between semi-custom and volume builder commissions is in the architectural changes your client contracts for.

Those changes are contracted separately and are usually paid before construction begins. Additionally, if your client cancels the contract after construction starts, the funds paid in advance for the changes are non-refundable. You must understand and communicate a builder's refund policy to your clients. In the case of semi-custom changes, the cost of making architectural changes can be substantial.

Client Registration

My final point is to repeat what I have already stated: you are the only person who cares about your commission. Register your client with the builder during your first visit to the model home. Then, if your client decides to contract with the builder to construct their new home, you must confirm, in writing, your commission amount, including the cost of the house, as well as any options and architectural changes. Like multi-family and custom builders, your commission is negotiable.

CHAPTER THREE KEY TAKEAWAYS

Chapter Three provides an overview of the key aspects you need to know when thinking about partnering with a semi-custom home builder. To reinforce your understanding of the material in this chapter, take a few minutes to answer the following three questions? Answering these key takeaways will strengthen your understanding of the chapter's main ideas and aid your ongoing learning about working and partnering with the new home builder community.

1. What spoke to you most about this chapter?

2. What insight in these pages made the most significant impression on you?

3. How will you take what you have learned in this chapter, and put it into action in your pursuit of new home sales?

Chapter Four

Volume Home Builders

A VOLUME HOME BUILDER builds houses using a collection of pre-designed floor plans. They focus on construction and purchasing efficiencies to deliver cost-effective housing solutions. Volume builders, also called production builders, can be local, regional, or national businesses. Many national volume home builders are publicly traded companies that build homes in hundreds of communities across the United States. Local production builders specialize in building in a particular community or area. A regional production builder builds across a state or group of states.

Because a volume builder has taken responsibility for planning, permitting, and organizing the house's construction, your clients will have fewer headaches regarding the building process. Almost every production builder has a construction process that eliminates unexpected issues. Due to their volume, production builders negotiate advantageous pricing for building materials.

Since a production builder buys lots from a developer or, in some situations, develops the land themselves, they have a say in what community amenities are included, such as walking and bike trails, playgrounds, and, if the community is large enough, a community pool, pickleball, and tennis courts. These amenities have long-lasting value and increase the home's worth over time.

When your client tours a home in a volume builder's community, the builder will have built a model home or a series of display houses to experience. During the tour, the builder's agent will explain which home features are standard and which are optional. A production builder may include $100,000 or more in optional or structural changes and designer upgrades. The purpose is to give your client a visual representation of what is available.

Most volume builders offer 5 to 7 house choices, each with 3 to 4 alternate exterior elevations. One elevation may be brick and siding, another stone and siding, and a third a combination of brick, stone, and siding. A production builder will also change the roof elevation to give the home a different look. Each elevation is offered at a different price, and production builders adhere to a policy of not repeating the same elevation side by side or across the street. The policy may also include color choices in brick, stone, siding, and shutters. This course of action is to protect your client's future investments.

To select options and colors, a volume builder will offer one of three choices, they are:

- **<u>Builder-owned design center</u>**: A large national volume builder may offer buyers a designated space to select from various appliances, countertops, carpeting, flooring, cabinetry, plumbing fixtures, and other features. In addition to providing a location away from the model home, a home designer will assist the client. The builder pays for this service.

- **<u>Outside design firm</u>**: Many volume builders offer design assistance from a company that specializes in helping clients make color and option selections. The builder typically covers the cost of this service.

- **<u>On-site builder agent</u>**: A smaller local volume home builder often limits a client's color and option choices by offering pre-designed color and option packages. The packages may include interior and exterior selections. In this situation, the client cannot change the color or options. This service is provided at no charge.

The on-site agent will review the builder's interior and exterior design policy during a client's first or second visit. The first and second options identified above offer your client the most flexibility and personalization, while the third option limits decision-making but provides the most cost-effective approach.

The good news for you and your clients is that volume builders construct cost-conscious houses of all shapes and sizes, including single-family homes, townhouses, rental properties, zero-lot-line homes, and condos. They build for families seeking their first home, clients who want more space as their lives change, and families looking to downsize. A production builder has much to offer your client; financial strength is the most crucial reason to consider a production builder.

Volume Builder Pricing

Prices for production homes vary according to location, building practices, quality materials, standard features, and buyer demand. Therefore, it is recommended that you conduct research when choosing a production builder. Later in this book, you will be asked to investigate builders to identify why one volume builder is more expensive than another, even though they are building in the same community. With this information, it will be easier for you to compare and contrast competing builders.

Regarding volume builder pricing, the more construction, options, and standard feature information you secure from your client's builder of choice and the builders they compete with, the better advice you can offer your client. Researching a builder's pricing is the difference that matters when selecting which builder to refer to your client.

PROS AND CONS OF VOLUME HOME BUILDERS

Pros:

- **Cost efficiency**: One of the benefits of building with a production builder is their competitive prices. The nature of a volume builder means that their houses cost less due to the purchase of materials in bulk and the absence of a need to order specialized products. Their streamlined construction processes and standardized designs contribute to quicker building timelines and reduced labor costs, translating into a more affordable option for your clients.

- **Purchase security**: Building with a production builder ensures clients get what they pay for. Having pre-designed floor plans and offering model homes confirms that you and your client know exactly what they are purchasing when signing a builder agreement. If a dispute arises, your client can refer to the model home, the standard feature list, and the agreement for guidance.

- **<u>Quick turnaround</u>**: If time is of the essence, a volume builder may be the best option for your client. As part of their marketing strategy, they construct inventory homes, which may be either wholly or partially finished. No changes are possible when the house is finished, but your client can choose some colors and options if the home is under construction. The potential changes depend on what stage of construction the house is in.

Cons:

- **<u>Limited personalization</u>**: Although volume builders offer a wide range of pre-designed floor plans and standard and structural options, customization is limited. A volume builder may not be the best choice if your clients have specific requirements or have a distinct vision for their home.

- **<u>Less involvement</u>**: Communication with a volume builder is limited to the on-site salesperson and construction superintendent. If your client requires daily or weekly construction updates, there may be better choices than a volume builder.

Remind your client that the average community construction superintendent manages around twelve houses at a time. If clients notice a construction issue, instruct them to report the problem to the on-site salesperson, who will then communicate it to the community construction supervisor.

JUST LOOKING

Volume builders are a valuable segment of the new home construction industry. However, not every production builder is the same. They will share similarities, but also have differences. To build a successful new home sales business, it is essential to understand these key differences. As I have written several times, introducing a client to a builder amounts to a referral. Unless you can communicate what makes one builder different, you should withhold your endorsement until you have experienced what makes your builder of choice worthy of your recommendation. Consider the following story, which illustrates why I believe it is essential to experience a builder firsthand before making a referral.

A home builder had retained me to conduct a two-hour CE class in one of their model homes. The builder provided a continental breakfast, offered door prizes, took the agents on a tour of the model home, and, if time permitted, escorted them on a community tour, all at no cost.

The class took place in the model's family room. The setting was intimate, and the students were encouraged to participate by asking questions. One of the agents asked a very defensive question about the builder's on-site salesperson and their involvement. I asked for some background information so I could better understand the question. The agent explained that she and her clients were driving through the community looking at existing homes; her client asked if they might stop at the model home for a quick look at a new home. Upon entering the model, the builder's salesperson rose to greet them. The agent explained they were *"Just looking"* and would be in and out quickly. The salesperson said, *"Great, let's go."* The agent said, *"That won't be necessary; we prefer to tour the home alone. If we have questions, I will let you know."*

At this point, I asked, *"Is there a reason you didn't want the builder's salesperson involved?"* She shrugged and said, *"My client was 'just looking,' and I felt we would be wasting the salesperson's time."* I acknowledged that I understood, and then I asked if she had ever visited the model home and if she was familiar with pricing, lot availability, building times, financing options, and other details. She responded, "*No.*" I asked if she felt that information would be helpful to her client since they had demonstrated an interest in new construction by wanting to stop at the model for a "*Quick look.*" This question caught her attention because she was focused solely on resale. She had not considered the possibility of new construction, but her client had thought about it and was curious enough to want to experience what the builder had to offer.

The circumstances I just described happen every day to new home salespeople. A Realtor stops at the model home for a "*Quick look*" to see the model home, but not to experience it with the one person who has all the answers to a client's questions. Don't be the agent who misses the opportunity to be different.

When you visit a model home, let the builder's salesperson guide you through the house. Let them highlight the home's standard, optional, and designer upgrades and any structural options the builder has included. Ask questions, and if you like what you hear and see, take the next step by requesting updates on sales, inventory homes, newly released lots, and changes in financing programs. Most importantly, ask the builder's salesperson to consider you if a client is interested in buying new construction, has a house to sell, and is not represented.

Once you understand the builders' benefits, you can confidently and without reservation offer your client a referral. You earn your client's trust and become a friend of the builder, and with this friendship come advantages. These advantages will be discussed throughout this book.

COMPENSATION

When working with volume builders, you can earn commission and additional compensation through various methods, including commission, bonuses, and incentive programs. Here's a more detailed breakdown:

Commission

Volume builders budget for Realtor commissions in their house costs, which are then split between you and your broker. Your commission is considered earned when you are deemed to be the procuring cause of the sale. To be regarded as the procuring cause, you must register as your client's agent during your first visit to the model home, or via the internet, and possibly by phone. I recommend verifying with the on-site salesperson which form of registration is acceptable as proof of Realtor and client registration. A registration usually remains valid for 90 days.

Procuring cause disputes often arise when you fail to register your client with the builder. In a commission dispute with the builder or another Realtor, the builder refers to three factors:

1. **Introduction of the buyer**: This factor examines who introduced the buyer to the builder. If the dispute is between two real estate agents, the Realtor who first brought the buyer's attention to the builder or initiated discussions is considered the agent of record. Suppose a home buyer visits the builder without a real estate agent on the first visit. In that case, the builder is not obligated to include the buyer's agent on the sales agreement because they are not considered the procuring cause.

2. **Efforts of the parties**: This factor assesses the different efforts to facilitate the sale. The agent who puts in significant effort, such as

actively promoting the builder and their homes, may be deemed the agent of record.

3. **Intent and Agreement:** This factor considers the intent and any written or verbal contracts (such as Realtor registration) regarding the commission. A clear understanding or agreement on the commission would significantly impact the dispute.

Bonus Programs

Many volume builders offer bonus programs and other financial incentives to encourage Realtors to work with them. A good example of a monetary incentive is a builder's 3/4/5 bonus program. The program operates as follows: for the first sale, the agent receives a 3% commission; for the second sale, a 4% commission; and for every sale thereafter, a 5% commission. The bonus program can be offered monthly, quarterly, or annually. When researching builders, I recommend conversing with the on-site agent about the type of incentive program provided to encourage real estate agents to work with them.

Non-Commission Bonuses

Incentives can include point-system raffles for prizes, thank-you gifts, or other rewards designed to build long-term relationships between builders and agents. A company I worked with for many years held an annual party celebrating agents who sold their homes. During the celebration, the agents received gifts, and those who reached a sales goal set by the builder were awarded an all-expense-paid trip to a foreign destination.

As you can see, most volume builders recognize the value of working with real estate agents and actively cultivate these relationships to increase sales. So, when considering which builders to partner with, I want you to consider the following:

- **<u>Commission structure</u>**: Production builders typically pay a commission ranging from 2% to 3% of the home's purchase price. Please check with the on-site agent if the home's purchase price includes options and structural upgrades.

- **<u>Co-op policies</u>**: Volume builders will have written policies that outline how commissions and bonuses are earned, including a strict Realtor and Client registration policy. Additionally, talk with your broker about the rewards and incentives you receive from a builder. Most states have specific guidelines for reporting bonuses and incentives to the broker and client.

- **<u>Negotiable commissions</u>**: The commission rate will be determined by the specific agreement between you and the builder.

One final note: builders who actively promote Realtor relationships often see a high percentage of their sales facilitated by real estate agents, with many builders I am familiar with reporting that seventy percent of their sales involve real estate agents.

Working with builders who want your business can benefit you if you follow their policies for co-op sales. To understand these policies, speak with the on-site salesperson and request copies of their co-op policies.

Additionally, consult with your broker to determine the proper reporting procedure for any commissions or incentives received from the builder.

<u>*CHAPTER FOUR KEY TAKEAWAYS*</u>

Chapter Four provides an overview of the key aspects you need to know when thinking about partnering with a volume home builder. To reinforce your understanding of the material in this chapter, take a few minutes to answer the following three questions? Answering these key takeaways will strengthen your understanding of the chapter's main ideas and aid your ongoing learning about working and partnering with the new home builder community.

1.   What spoke to you most about this chapter?

2.   What insight in these pages made the most significant impression on you?

3.   How will you take what you have learned in this chapter, and put it into action in your pursuit of new home sales?

Choosing A Home Builder Type to Partner With

S O FAR, I HAVE written about four new home builder types, they are:

1. Multi-family home builder.

2. Custom home builder.

3. Semi-custom home builder.

4. Volume home builder.

Each builder type offers pros and cons that should be considered before deciding which one might best help build your new home sales business. For most Realtors reading this book, I believe the volume or production home builder is the right choice. So, this book focuses on partnering with the volume or production home builder community. However, my ideas throughout the book can be applied to any builder. If you follow my advice, you will be amazed at the results you achieve, regardless of the builder you partner with.

A quick disclaimer about this book: volume builders are not all alike. The many insights I offer in the following chapters will apply to the majority of production builders. Still, I want you to expect differences from one volume builder to the next. Throughout the remaining chapters, I will remind you to talk with the on-site salesperson to understand what these differences might be. It is these differences that make one volume builder a better choice for you and your clients.

Now, let's explore how to work with and connect to the Volume Home Builder Community.

How to Select The Right Volume Builder

Choosing the right volume builder, whether it be a national, regional or local is a big decision. The following represents the factors that should play a role in your selection.

Reputation

The reputations of large national volume home-building companies may vary from state to state. Because of this, a local volume home builder may have an advantage due to their relationships with community leaders and municipal employees, including those who approve building and construction permits, and their likely involvement in community affairs.

Another aspect of reputation is financial strength. This is where the large national builder may have an advantage. The money used to build their homes typically comes from lines of credit established by the national builder's corporate office. This benefit provides your client with peace of mind regarding whether the builder has the necessary funds to construct and complete the house and whether the builder can offer post-closing services.

Home Owner Satisfaction

Besides reviewing online opinions and complaints about local and national builders, be sure to ask for references from people who have recently built homes with them. Ask if they are satisfied with the quality of their homes and if they have experienced any complaints regarding communication, quality, repairs, or other issues.

Mortgage and Title Company Options

What mortgage and title company options does a local builder offer versus a national builder? Does the builder own the mortgage or title company, or do they have a list of preferred mortgage and title companies to which they refer your client? Is there a significant difference in mortgage rates and terms if the builder owns the company? Does the builder offer incentives to use either the builder-owned or builder-preferred mortgage or title company?

Variety of House Plans

National builders offer a variety of pre-designed house plans, and their product offerings will change due to location, lot size, pricing, HOA, and developer requirements. Additionally, they utilize a standardized approach that enables them to complete homes quickly and at an affordable price.

Local builders may offer more plan choices but at a higher price, and with additional choices come slower build times. The local builder may focus its marketing efforts on a specific buyer, which limits its flexibility. In contrast, a national builder will offer various design options, depending on the community plan requirements (single-family detached, condos, zero-lot line, townhouses), which appeal to a broader market.

Construction Quality

Quality is a crucial factor, whether you use a national or local builder, and can vary based on the skill and expertise of the construction crew. When you visit model homes, look for signs that may indicate quality issues, but remember that a model home will differ from the home your client purchases. A model home typically includes 100,000 dollars or more in options, design, and structural upgrades, which may mask construction issues.

The best representation of a local or national builder's quality may be found in either houses under construction or finished inventory homes. So, be sure you and your client visit multiple inventory homes to experience a builder's quality of construction. An additional benefit is that an inventory home offers limited options; therefore, it accurately represents what your client purchases.

Resale Value

Ultimately, all homes will be resold. Examine the resale homes currently for sale in the community and compare the sales prices of the national builder with those of the local builder. Which homes have appreciated the most?

Communication

How easy is it to talk to someone who knows what's happening during the construction of your client's new home? Although you and your client may receive plenty of attention when deciding whether to build a house, will the staff be as eager to talk during construction? If you and your client choose a national builder, you may work with a staff of people during the sales, construction, mortgage, and closing processes. Local builders are more likely to assign one or two contacts who will help you navigate the entire process.

Features and Upgrades

It's not unusual for national builders to limit upgrades to simplify the building process. That is not to say they don't offer structural options to alter the home layout, but those modifications will be limited. If your client wants the flexibility to enlarge their family room or turn a home office into a guest suite, a local builder may be the better choice.

As an added benefit, national builders will provide a design center and a designer to assist clients in selecting cabinets, countertops, appliances, flooring, lighting, and paint colors, among other options. However, when the upgrade or options are added, you must remind your clients that additional costs may be involved. To summarize, local and national builders can deliver the personalization your client wants, but at what cost?

Problem-Solving

Ask local and national builders how construction issues are addressed and how soon a client can expect an answer or resolution. Ask them if they have a third-party warranty or if they are self-insured. Ask whether they employ a designated service department to handle customer issues. The answer to these questions will dictate which builder, national or local, has the advantage in after-closing problem-solving.

The simple fact is that whether your client is building with a local volume builder or a national volume builder, there will be construction issues that need to be resolved. It is not whether a construction issue will happen, but when one develops. Preparing your client for these occurrences is best achieved by partnering with a builder with customer service policies and procedures to handle problems efficiently and on time.

Volume Home Builder Benefits

Ultimately, selecting a local, regional, or national home builder often boils down to the specific benefits each offers. What follows are the potential benefits you may encounter when deciding whether to work exclusively with one builder or a combination of builders, including multi-family, custom, semi-custom, and production builders. Those potential benefits are:

- Builder and Realtor partnerships.

- Home design choices.

- Builder and client meetings.

- Builder services.

Each of the identified benefits are explored in the following four chapters. Read each chapter carefully. The reasons to choose one volume builder over another are set forth within these chapters. Remember, not all volume builders are alike. There are differences, and those are discussed in the following chapters.

CHAPTER FIVE KEY TAKEAWAYS

Chapter Five provides an overview of the key aspects you need to know when choosing a home builder type to partner with. To reinforce your understanding of the material in this chapter, take a few minutes to answer the following three questions? Answering these key takeaways will strengthen your understanding of the chapter's main ideas and aid your ongoing learning about working and partnering with the new home builder community.

1. What spoke to you most about this chapter?

2. What insight in these pages made the most significant impression on you?

3. How will you take what you have learned in this chapter, and put it into action in your pursuit of new home sales?

Managing Volume Builder Partnerships

DEPENDING ON THE VOLUME builder's size, as many as nine people will partner with you in the sale, construction, mortgage, design, settlement, and after-closing service of a new home purchase. Job titles and responsibilities of those nine people are listed below, along with your role for each partner.

SALESPERSON PARTNER

Responsibilities include the following:

- Ask discovery and qualifying questions to help prospective buyers select a floor plan and options that meet their housing needs.

- Present the model home's standard features, structural upgrades, designer upgrades, options, and related benefits.

- Explain the builder's construction methods and benefits.

- Follow up with prospective clients via phone calls, text messages, and emails to gauge their level of interest.

- Maintain accurate records of all communications throughout the sales, construction, mortgage, color selection, and closing processes.

- Negotiate with the buyer the final price, including the house and options, to be presented to the builder for approval.

- Draft the sales agreement and addenda.

- Arrange for mortgage financing and a title company.

- Be available to handle any building issues from the start of construction to the closing.

Your Role

Your role initially is to provide the on-site salesperson with the reason for the visit. When the builder's agent understands your purpose, they can provide the critical information you need to determine if the homes, homesites, community, location, financing, and builder suit your client.

A salesperson wants to serve you, but that will not happen unless they understand your needs and intentions. Please do not hold back; open up to the salesperson and tell them precisely what you want to accomplish. Later in the book, I provide examples of how to set expectations for the builder, the on-site salesperson, and your client.

Now, let's be clear about the on-site salesperson. They are not all the same. Some will be outstanding, but many are satisfied to sit in the model home, welcome people when they arrive, let them look around, and, if necessary, be available to answer questions. In such situations, you must be the catalyst that draws out the builder's information on homes, homesites, community, location, and financing, thereby enabling you and your client to make an informed decision.

CONSTRUCTION SUPERVISOR PARTNER

Responsibilities include the following:

- Manage community new home construction utilizing the builder's scheduling system from foundation to completion.

- Assists in ordering all necessary materials for the construction of the house.

- Supervise on-site construction crews, including scheduling sub-contractors and suppliers as needed.

- Monitor all daily trade functions: timeliness, work quality, and completion.

- Resolving day-to-day problems on the job site, inspecting all work during construction to ensure compliance with plans and specifications.

- Perform quality inspections after each phase of construction is complete.

- Answer customer questions about possible construction issues throughout the building process.

- Manage customer meetings before, during, and after construction is completed.

- Maintain the appearance and upkeep of the model home and community.

- Meet weekly with model home salespeople to discuss customer construction concerns and provide resolutions that can be communicated to the homebuyer.

Your Involvement During Construction

Your involvement during construction will vary depending on the builder's policies and procedures and the extent to which your client wishes you to be involved. Therefore, discussing your participation level with the on-site salesperson and client before construction begins is recommended.

A question to your client might be something like this: ***"I am ready, willing, and able to be involved in the construction of your new home; tell me, how much involvement you would like me to have?"*** After you ask the question, pause and let your client consider their answer. In my experience, your client will answer your question by asking about your past experiences. Here is when you can provide the reasons your involvement might be needed. The two most common reasons are community construction supervisor meetings and proper handling of construction issues.

Your Involvement and Its Limitations

Community Construction Supervisor Meeting

By attending customer meetings you provide additional eyes and ears, ensuring clear and understandable communication between your client and the builder regarding the home's construction, maintenance, and care. However, it is not your decision to make. The decision belongs to your client. Discuss your involvement during the builder meetings with them. When they understand your value, they are likely to want you to be involved.

Customer Construction Issues

Exercise caution when addressing customer issues. I recommend letting your client know that you are available to discuss a construction issue and will offer advice and opinions on how the problem might be addressed. Then, it is best to clarify that they, not you, communicate the issue directly to the person responsible for handling customer construction concerns. In most volume builder situations, the builder's on-site agent is that person.

Client Communication with Construction Supervisor

Instruct your client to email the on-site salesperson a detailed description of the construction issue, including photos. Ask your client to close the email with a request for a written response on the action to be taken. By doing this, they create a paper trail and respect the salesperson's time spent selling. This is a win-win-win for your client, the salesperson, and the construction supervisor.

Ask your client to copy you on written communication with the on-site salesperson or builder.

Your Role

A question that might help clarify your role with the on-site salesperson and community construction manager is: ***"I want my client to have an excellent new home experience. What can I do to make that happen?"***

Listen carefully to the response, and follow up with additional questions related to the answer. By asking questions to clarify your participation during construction, you demonstrate your commitment to working closely with the on-site salesperson and construction supervisor to ensure your client receives the type of positive new home experience they deserve. Please notify them if you or your client encounters any construction issues; you have instructed your client to contact them directly for resolution.

IN-OFFICE SALES ADMINISTRATOR PARTNER

Responsibilities include the following:

- Review purchase agreements for accuracy.

- Post-sales, cancellations, transfers, and closings.

- Scan and distribute executed purchase agreements to Realtor, buyers, and mortgage companies.

- Create house files for all new purchase agreements.

- Manage and distribute mortgage status reports to sales staff.

- Update unsold inventory dates, loan status, and contract pricing as needed.

- Update all base sales prices and options to sales staff.

- Gather weekly model home traffic and distribute it to designated end users.

Your Role

As stated, this is an administrative position in the sales office. You will have no direct contact with them, but they provide a valuable service by handling all administrative responsibilities related to purchase agreements. Your responsibility for the purchase agreement ends once the builder ratifies the sale.

HOME BUYER CONCIERGE PARTNER

Responsibilities include the following:

- Serve as the home buyers' point of contact once escrow has been opened throughout the mortgage, design, construction, and closing.

- Set clear and concise expectations with home buyers that support builder policies and procedures.

- Provide home buyers with relevant, timely updates on their build status and help answer all questions and concerns.

- Coordinate introductions and meetings between the home buyer, mortgage, design center, construction, and closing departments.

Your Role

You are likely familiar with the term *"Concierge"* in the context of resorts or large hotels, but did you know that many large-volume builders also offer concierge services to their homebuyers? Once an agreement has been reached between the builder and the home buyer, they are assigned an individual who will be their sole point of contact for mortgage, option, and design selections, construction, and settlement. The goal of the concierge is to provide the home buyer with a personalized and exceptional home-buying experience, focusing on timely communication and superior customer service.

The home buyer concierge is a customer-centered service, so your role with them will be limited. I recommend speaking with the on-site salesperson to fully understand the concierge service's benefits and determine how you will be kept informed as your client progresses through the various stages of the construction and settlement process.

In-Office Closing Administrator Partner

Responsibilities include the following:

- Collaborate with home buyers, providing them with clear communication to ensure a seamless closing experience.

- Review closing documents and convey settlement instructions correctly to all parties involved.

- Support home buyers, on-site salespersons, community construction supervisors, and Realtors with informative communication about closing status.

- Enhance the closing day experience by continually communicating with the on-site construction supervisor to produce a smooth transition from the final home inspection and orientation to the closing table.

- Upload all closing documents immediately following settlement to ensure timely funding of home purchases.

Your Role

As stated, this is an in-office administrative position responsible for closing. You will have no direct contact with them. Still, they provide a valuable service in handling communications between the office, the construction supervisor, the on-site salesperson, the home buyer, and the title company. Any communication regarding the closing status will be handled through the on-site salesperson, who will be in constant contact with the closing administrator. The closing administrator, in turn, will maintain continuous communication with the community construction supervisor regarding the construction status.

INTERIOR & EXTERIOR DESIGN PARTNER

Responsibilities include the following:

- Schedule design appointments with home buyers.

- Assist home buyers with color and product selections.

- Enter selections and additional options purchased during design meetings into the home buyer's online file.

- Prepare decorator selection package for builder's inventory homes, including color and option selections.

- Meet vendors to review new product offerings.

- Maintain design center samples, signage, and option pricing.

- Prepare sales reports for the builder's marketing managers.

- Research the latest new build designs and trends.

Your Role

A significant advantage of purchasing a new home is the opportunity for your clients to select options and finishes that reflect their personal design preferences. Several factors must be considered, including the options to choose, the structural changes to implement, budgeting, and how the selected options and finishes will impact resale value.

Your client may need assistance during selection in the following four areas:

1. Budgeting.

2. Structural changes.

3. Options.

4. Resale value.

The following explores each area:

Budgeting

Buying a home is a significant purchase; it typically includes a base price, optional upgrades, and potential structural modifications. Let your client know that the average home buyer will add ten to twelve percent to the base price in options and structural upgrades. Therefore, a home with a base price of $400,000 will have a final cost of around $450,000. The ten-to-twelve percent option increase is a good rule of thumb. If your client keeps that percentage in mind as they tour new builds, they will have no difficulty staying within their housing budget.

Additionally, most volume builders either have preferred lenders and title companies they refer to or have an affiliated business arrangement with a builder-owned lender and title company. To encourage your client to use these services, the builder will offer an incentive to offset the cost. These option incentives are only available if your client uses the builder's mortgage and title services.

Structural Changes

Inform your clients that if they wish to add pre-designed structural or plumbing changes, they must make these selections during the sales process, as these changes affect the city's or county's building permit requirements. Some builders will allow minor electrical changes before installing drywall, such as relocating an electrical outlet or adding coaxial, or fiber optic cables. However, they will not agree to opening walls after completing the drywall phase of construction.

Options

Advise your clients to consider upgrading floors, cabinets, and counter-tops. I suggest these three areas because they are subject to daily wear and tear. I am not suggesting that they buy the highest builder upgrade; I recommend that your client not settle for the builder's standard flooring, cabinets, and countertops.

Furthermore, I suggest discussing with your client the possibility of making some cosmetic changes after moving into the home, such as changing paint colors, adding landscaping, updating light and plumbing fixtures, enhancing rooms by installing crown molding and chair rails, and even replacing appliances. By encouraging your clients to do some sweat equity, they can save money and extend their housing budget.

Resale Value

Building a new home is one of the best investments someone can make. Like any investment, your client needs to plan for the future. Life, as you know, has plenty of twists and turns, and clients cannot predict when they will need to make a change. Even if they tell you this new build will be their forever home, they still need to keep home resale in mind. And that means making informed choices and options that will stand the test of time.

Advise your client to keep flooring, cabinetry, and countertops neutral, while showcasing their personal color preferences through wall colors, rugs, furniture, window coverings, and other decorative elements. I suggest this because these things can be changed without requiring a renovation.

Design Center Visit

A final recommendation is scheduling a visit to the builder's design center. The purpose of this visit is to experience what your client is experiencing. You will see firsthand what finishes and selections are available. You can ask questions so you can answer your client's questions. To accomplish this visit, you will need the builder's permission. Some builders will embrace the idea, while others might be hesitant. That is understandable because very few, if any, Realtors will make this request.

Throughout this book, I have written that there are times when you can demonstrate to the builder's salesperson and to the builder that you are different. This is one of those opportunities.

TITLE COMPANY PARTNER

Responsibilities include the following:

- Completing a title search.

- Closing the transaction.

- Issuing title insurance.

Your Role

Although the services offered and fees charged by title companies across most of the country are standardized, their operational practices vary. As your brokerage and agents differ in operating standards and styles, so do title companies. However, the one thing all title companies have in common is that they serve as a neutral third party.

If you believe the builder's preferred or owned title company is reputable, competitive in fees, conveniently located, and consistently prioritizes a client's interests, then referring to the builder's title service is warranted. However, your client must understand that they are not obligated to use the builder's service; you recommend it based on past experiences with the title company. Additionally, if the builder offers an incentive, your client must understand that the incentive will not apply to another title company.

Lastly, I suggest you discuss your attendance at the closing with your client. In my experience, your client will likely tell you it is unnecessary, but let them decide.

Mortgage Company Partner

Responsibilities include the following:

- Assist clients in understanding various mortgage products, their associated interest rates, and the implications of each product.

- Explain the application process and aid the client in choosing the loan that best suits their financial situation.

- Responsible for collecting and evaluating financial information from applicants.

- Oversee the preparation and submission of necessary documentation for loan applications.

- Maintain communication with the borrower to ensure timely loan approval and closing.

- Coordinate with underwriters for a smooth and efficient application process.

- Maintain relationships with real estate agents by informing them about the mortgage approval status.

Your Role

A client who rushes to find a lender before checking with you is missing out on one of your most valuable services. Your role in finding the correct financing for your client is crucial to the successful close of escrow.

While the lender is critical during the application process and when it comes to funding the loan, you are the point person helping your client prepare for the mortgage application. Too many clients see your role as a tour guide to help them find their dream home. However, most would-be home buyers are unaware that agents will not begin touring properties until a mortgage is pre-approved, revealing that the buyer has the income and good credit to purchase.

Initially, you will want your client to secure the two most critical documents to ensure a smooth loan application: a credit report and a credit score. Credit reports are accessible from AnnualCreditReport.com; while credit scores may incur a small fee, the investment is worthwhile.

A client's credit report will reveal if any errors or problems could affect their application. While your client may not want to share the report directly, you can help them develop a strategy to improve the score, correct errors, or take other steps to improve the report before a builder's lender takes the mortgage application.

Beyond good credit, you must discuss with your client the need for them to verify employment, income, down payment sources, and other qualifying factors.

When your client has all the documentation necessary to apply for a loan, you must clarify that they can shop for the best rate and terms. Still, your recommendation does warrant some consideration, especially if they are considering new home construction.

Critical Client and Realtor Discussion Points

Buyer Representation Agreement

On or after client has been pre-approved for a mortgage, you are now ready to begin exploring new and resale homes. However, I want to remind you to secure a signed Buyer's Representation Agreement.

Earlier in this chapter, I wrote that you are the only one who cares about your compensation; therefore, your client must sign a Buyer's Representation Agreement to protect yourself. The agreement specifies the percentage of the sales price you will be paid upon successfully closing a property. The builder will pay you a commission if your client purchases a new home, and the seller will pay you a commission if your client buys a resale. If either the buyer or seller refuses to pay the commission, then your client is responsible for your commission.

I mention this because some on-site builder agents might suggest to your client, *"If a Realtor had not represented you, I would be able to offer a discount on the purchase price."* While this is unethical, it does happen.

Obtain a signed Buyer's Representation Agreement from your client to shield yourself from unprincipled salespeople. If your client refuses to sign, you have a choice; I hope you make the right choice and protect yourself before organizing and scheduling home tours.

Remember that sales are like buses: miss one, wait a short time, and catch the next one.

Pre-Approval Letter from Another Lender

Your client obtained a pre-approval letter from a reputable lender, separate from the builder. While touring new and resale homes, you find a new home that satisfies all your client's needs and wants. Sometimes the builder will have a list of preferred lenders they recommend. The builder offers an incentive to encourage home buyers to use the lender.

Your client now faces a decision. Should they opt for the builder's preferred lender and earn the incentive, or should they stick with their original lender, who provided the pre-approval letter?

Before starting your home search, consider discussing the possibility of receiving a builder's options incentive if you use the builder's preferred or owned mortgage company. Inform them that while the incentive is attractive, it may not be the best choice because the mortgage rate and fees may be higher than those they have already secured through pre-approval. I suggest that they take the time to compare the builder's mortgage against the lender who has provided the pre-approval letter. They may learn that the outside lender is the better choice and will save them money over the life of the loan. They may also realize that the builder's mortgage is competitive, and the option incentive will allow them to add upgrades they would not have been able to afford otherwise.

A mortgage is a big decision. Your role in this decision will earn you the right to request a referral, and you are aware of the vital importance of referrals to your overall business success.

Construction Timelines

When considering a new home, your client has two options: purchase a completed inventory home or a to-be-built home. Financing a builder's inventory home that is complete or nearly complete is similar to securing a mortgage for a resale home. However, purchasing a to-be-built home can be challenging because new home construction typically takes six to eight months to complete. As you know, mortgage rates fluctuate daily and can change significantly between when your client signs a purchase agreement and when the home is completed.

If your client elects to build from the ground up, suggest they consider a long-term rate lock. Some builder lenders offer a six, nine, or even twelve-month lock against an increase in the mortgage rate. Additionally, they may provide a float-down option that allows your client to take advantage of lower mortgage rates if interest rates drop after the rate lock is issued.

Once again, your advice on construction timelines and mortgage rate locks sets you apart from other Realtors. A decision to refer you to family and friends may be as simple as your advice throughout the home purchasing process. It often begins with information about construction timelines or mortgage rate locks.

INTERNET SALES COORDINATOR

Responsibilities include the following:

- Present builder information to prospective customers online about quick move-in homes, communities, financing options, and current builder incentives.

- Provide prompt follow-up via email, text, live chat, and phone.

- Schedule customer visits to communities and expedite a smooth transition to the on-site salesperson(s).

- Maintain and update digital and community reference material.

- Send monthly updates to online inquiries regarding new product offerings, available inventory homes, price changes, promotions, incentives, and new community and product offerings.

- Monitor community websites to maintain accuracy.

- Attend and participate in sales meetings and future community start-up meetings.

Your Role

The Internet sales coordinator position is quickly becoming a builder's best salesperson. They have the answers to questions about builders' locations, pricing, products, financing, quick move-in opportunities, incentives, and promotions. Prospective homebuyers appreciate the position because the answers they provide can either lead them to visit a community to learn more or eliminate a community and move to a location that best fits their needs. This saves the prospective home buyer and the on-site salesperson time. It is a win-win situation for everyone, and can be a winning situation for you.

Consider the following scenario: a new client is interested in touring new home communities. They have been pre-approved for a home up to $400,000. They have a growing family and are looking for a four-bedroom house with a three-car garage. They also want a home office and an open floor plan. You have a choice: go to your local Multiple Listing Service

(MLS) and begin a search, or call a builder's online sales coordinator. If you are smart, and I know you are, you call the online sales coordinator.

I have several suggestions that will make your call welcome. They are:

- Develop a relationship with the online sales coordinator by making an introductory phone call.

- Communicate that you want to build your real estate business by offering new home construction.

- Ask what buyer information would be most helpful to narrow down a home search.

- Request to be included in builder email communications that update online customers on price changes, new product offerings, promotions, incentives, and quick-move-in opportunities.

- Follow up with a phone call or email to thank the online coordinator for their help and express your interest in working with them shortly.

Since 2013, when I began teaching Realtors how to connect with and work within the new home build community, the number one question I have been asked is, ***"Where can I find new home information?"*** Back then, the online sales coordinator position did not exist. If you wanted new home information, you had to search the MLS or get in your car and drive until you found a community that met your clients' home-buying criteria. It was not a good use of your time, so more often than not, you take the path of least resistance and focus your sales efforts on resale.

Fortunately, things have changed, and that is no longer the case today. You can submit a housing inquiry via chat or email through a builder's website. Alternatively, if you have followed my suggestions and developed a relationship with the online sales coordinator, you can place a phone call directly from the comfort of your home office. You quickly learn about the available homes, including the options, purchase price, incentives, financing options, and whether the house has a Realtor bonus.

Earlier, I wrote about builders offering home buyers a concierge service; the online sales coordinator is your concierge service. Builders are offering you a better way to service your client; begin contacting online sales coordinators today and take advantage of this time-saving and money-making opportunity.

CHAPTER SIX KEY TAKEAWAYS

Chapter Six provides an overview of the key aspects you need to know when managing volume home builder partnerships. To reinforce your understanding of the material in this chapter, take a few minutes to answer the following three questions? Answering these key takeaways will strengthen your understanding of the chapter's main ideas and aid your ongoing learning about working and partnering with the new home builder community.

1. What spoke to you most about this chapter?

2. What insight in these pages made the most significant impression on you?

3. How will you take what you have learned in this chapter, and put it into action in your pursuit of new home sales?

Volume Builder House Designs

M ENTION THE TERM VOLUME builder to an architect, and there's a fair chance they might recoil. What they see in their mind's eye is mass-produced boxes. The reality is that volume builders' house designs have significantly changed since the 2008 housing crisis.

COMMUNITY HOUSE DESIGN & SELECTION PROCESS

Today's production builder houses are designed to meet current interior and exterior trends, such as open floor plans, plenty of natural light, high ceilings, well-appointed kitchens, ample storage spaces for clothing, garages big enough to store lawns and sports equipment, and elevations that include stone, brick, stucco, and, for many builders, maintenance-free siding.

You can find all the information regarding exterior design, standard building features, and structural options in the community brochure, which is distributed at the model home. However, you may need to learn how the builder selects and approves those house designs if a client has questions. What follows is the process a typical volume builder undertakes to make informed decisions about new home designs.

Location Selection

The search begins for a suitable tract of land. Once the builder selects a location, they start working with a developer. Frequently, the developer, with builder approval, will assemble several adjacent pieces of property purchased from different owners to create one large site that can accommodate various housing styles, ranging from single-family homes to townhomes to zero-lot-line dwellings, and in many cases, even custom and semi-custom homes.

At this point, the builder and developer will present a community plan to the local municipality for zoning approval. Depending on the jurisdiction and complexity of the development, this process can take several years to complete.

Design Committee

Once the community's zoning is approved, a design committee is comprised of on-site salespeople, marketing personnel, construction supervisors, and management. The committee engages with the builders' in-office architect or hires an outside architectural firm to design a series of homes that meet the committee's design criteria. This typically includes five to seven house plans with varying interior room layouts. Each design will have three to four different exterior elevations.

After several months of design development, the architect will meet with the committee to present recommended house designs. Exterior elevations and interior room layouts are reviewed, redlined, and returned to the architect for changes. After several meetings between the architect and the committee, a house series is approved and released to the builder's estimating department to determine selling prices.

Research

While the builders' estimating department accepts bids, the marketing department begins reviewing the new designs with local Realtors and home-buying prospects who have demonstrated an interest in the new community. The agents who attend are considered *"Friends of the Builder"* because they have successfully closed multiple homes built by the builder. Each house plan is presented, and attendees are asked to evaluate the interior room layout and exterior elevations for possible design flaws. House blueprints are redlined, and notes are taken describing the reason for the suggested modification. The blueprints and notes are then presented to the design committee for approval or dismissal.

Model and Inventory Home Construction

The developer has completed underground gas and electricity, the sewer and water lines are in place, and the streets are paved. The community is ready for new home construction. The first homes built are the approved new house designs. Several will become model homes, and the others will be inventory homes built for the market.

When framing is complete, the design committee will review each house to identify any room layout flaws that may have been missed during the review phase. The blueprints are then corrected and returned to the architect for plan updates.

Once plan revisions are complete, the marketing department sends the approved houses to a company specializing in brochure development. Drafts are prepared and sent back to marketing for approval. Following acceptance, the brochure is sent to the printer for printing and distribution to the on-site salesperson.

Cookie-Cutter Homes

The builder is ready to accept sales after several years of community development. You and your client have visited the model home, and they like the location; the homes and homesites are unique and tailored to their preferences, and pricing is within their budget. The only concern is that they have heard that volume builders construct houses that are all alike. They use the term *"Cookie-Cutter"* when describing a production builder community. It is not what they see in the community that you need to overcome; it is what they have heard.

Community Monotony Code

When faced with this concern, it's essential to highlight the protective measures builders have put into place. Encourage the on-site salesperson to review the builder's community monotony code with your client. This code protects your client's investment, as the builder mandates sufficient differences in house designs, color schemes, and exterior finishes, including brick, stone, siding, and roof design.

Here's a glimpse of how a monotony code might be structured:

- Homes of the same elevation may be built, provided at least one home of a different elevation is built in between. If the elevation is the same across the street, it must be one home over.

- The same exterior siding and masonry color may be installed, provided two homes of different color selections are built between them. If across the street, the same color must be two homes over.

- In cul-de-sac circles, all homes must be significantly different.

The monotony code is designed to protect your client's investment. However, it can also work against them if they delay their purchase and another buyer expresses interest in a similar color scheme or house design. Therefore, once the decision to buy is made, it's crucial to act swiftly. I recommend you persuade your client to sign an agreement and schedule a design meeting as soon as possible to avoid potential design and color conflicts with other buyers.

So, when you hear the word *"Cookie-Cutter"* or see doubt in your client's eyes when you mention touring a community that includes volume builders, take a few moments to walk your clients through a builder's new home design process. You might be surprised to learn that no one has ever taken the time to explain how a builder brings new home designs to market.

Knowledge of the new home design process gives you a deeper understanding of how builders select their new home community designs. Apply that understanding to alleviate your clients' fears, boost sales and income, and enhance your credibility as a new home sales expert.

Chapter Seven Key Takeaways

Chapter Seven provides an overview of the key aspects you need to know about how volume builders bring to market new home designs. To reinforce your understanding of the material in this chapter, take a few minutes to answer the following three questions? Answering these key takeaways will strengthen your understanding of the chapter's main ideas and aid your ongoing learning about working and partnering with the new home builder community.

1. What spoke to you most about this chapter?

2. What insight in these pages made the most significant impression on you?

3. How will you take what you have learned in this chapter, and put it into action in your pursuit of new home sales?

Volume Builder Construction Meetings

F OUR BUILDER AND CLIENT construction meetings are possible, depending on the volume builder's size. None of these meetings between your client and the builder is mandatory, but each serves a purpose. I strongly urge you to promote your client's attendance at each meeting. Additionally, inform your client that these meetings are scheduled according to the construction supervisor's schedule, not theirs.

The four possible builder and client construction meetings are as follows:

1. Pre-Construction Meeting.

2. Pre-Drywall Meeting.

3. Pre-Closing Inspection Meeting.

4. Pre-Closing Orientation Meeting.

Below is a review of what you and your client can expect during each meeting.

Pre-Construction Meeting

The pre-construction meeting takes place on the homesite and is your client's introduction to their construction supervisor. Following the introduction, the details of the home and home building process are reviewed, and your clients' questions are answered.

The construction supervisor will review the plot plan, which outlines the lot and indicates the home's location. The city or county establishes front yard setbacks and side yard requirements, and the builder must adhere to the community's approved standards.

The location of the lot easements is identified on the plan. If your client is a first-time buyer, the builder may explain that an easement is a right-of-way for utilities, such as power, cable, and internet lines. The respective companies could dig up that area without permission if their lines needed to be repaired or replaced.

Another important detail about house placement is reviewed: garage location. Some garages are placed on the right side of the house, while others are placed on the left. For proper drainage, builders prefer placing the garage on the high side of the lot. Nine times out of ten, this method of determining the location of the garage works best, but certain factors could require an alternate plan, such as:

- Relocation of the garage entrance to another street (most commonly occurs on corner lots).

- The garage placement was changed due to a utility location.

- Relocation of the garage placement due to personal preference.

Relocation due to personal preference may not be the best action, as the client's preferred garage location could negatively impact proper drainage. However, it is worth investigating if your client demonstrates a strong partiality to a particular garage location.

Additionally, the builder will discuss the placement of air conditioning units and other exterior equipment, the location of fences and sidewalks, and the selection and placement of landscaping materials, all included in the purchase price.

After that, the builder will discuss lot grading. A vital grading aspect is positioning swales around the house perimeter to keep water flowing away from the house and directed to the front or rear of the lot. Your client will be warned not to alter the lot drainage by building any obstruction that affects rainwater runoff. If the lot drainage is changed, it can affect the builder's warranty.

The house foundation is reviewed with suggestions. The most important ones are installing rain gutters (if not included as a standard feature) and a sprinkler system. The gutters will divert water from the house. The sprinkler system will keep the earth around the foundation moist enough to prevent it from drying out and causing openings, which could allow water to seep into those fissures, get underneath the foundation, and cause lifting or cracking.

The builder will further explain that some minor cracking in concrete is unavoidable. No repair will be made if the crack is within the performance standards outlined in the builder's limited warranty.

Next, the builder will review the house blueprint, including any structural upgrades and options added during the contract signing or the design meeting. For clarification purposes, the builder will review the standard feature sheet. Your client will be reminded that no changes can be made to the home after construction has started.

After that, the construction supervisor will review what to expect during the construction process. Your client is told that building a house requires many vendors and subcontractors to produce the final product. Each person depends on another person to finish their task before moving on to the next phase of the house. The builder will explain that they use an electronic tracking system and calendar to keep everyone on the same page, ensuring that things can proceed as scheduled.

However, building supply shortages, labor shortages, and weather delays can occur. Therefore, the builder will warn the client to expect something that might disrupt the building process, including events beyond the control of the construction supervisor. Your client will be reminded that everyone has the same goal: a finished home that the builder and your client will be proud of.

Finally, the builder will review the procedures for a construction issue. For most volume builders, this means bringing the problem to the attention of the on-site salesperson. The builder will explain that the on-site salesperson and construction supervisor meet weekly to discuss the status of every home under construction. Following the weekly meeting, the on-site salesperson will contact them by email, text, or phone with a solution that addresses their concerns.

Construction Site and Client Safety

A home's construction site can be dangerous. Therefore, advise your client to contact the on-site salesperson for authorization before coming to the house unannounced. Depending on what is under construction, they may be unable to go inside.

When they visit the construction site, they must always observe safety rules without exception and wear the appropriate personal protective equipment (PPE). Failure to abide by the builder's safety policies may result in your client being banned from the site until construction is complete or restricted from visiting the home only under the supervision of the construction supervisor. PPE is usually available at the model home center or the supervisor's construction trailer.

New Home Journal and Photo Album

Building a new home is an exciting and rewarding experience. Your client witnesses an empty lot transform into a bustling construction site, beginning with a foundation and progressing to framing, mechanical systems (including plumbing, electrical, and HVAC), drywall, painting, and finishing details on both the interior and exterior, culminating in a move-in-ready home. Each phase of construction offers new memories to cherish. In the excitement of it all, homebuyers often forget to take a moment to savor the experience.

Consider gifting your client a New Home Construction Journal, accompanied by a Photo Album and a Polaroid Camera. Both the camera and journal are readily available through Amazon, and I have seen Construction Journals available through Etsy that can be personalized with your client's name.

Building a new home is a journey filled with ups and downs; a picture and a few written thoughts will be much appreciated in the years to come as your client looks back on everything that made their new home possible.

Your Role

Your role during the Pre-Construction meetings is at the discretion of your client. First-time home buyers may want you to attend to observe and ask clarifying questions. In contrast, more experienced home buyers know what questions to ask if something the construction supervisor says needs clarification.

In Book Four of this series, *The New Home Construction Process*, I suggest assisting your clients during the Pre-Construction, Pre-Drywall, and Pre-Closing Inspection meetings. Therefore, if you wish to attend any of these meetings, you must demonstrate the value you bring to each meeting. Once your client understands your usefulness, I am sure you will be welcomed and encouraged to participate.

PRE-DRYWALL MEETING

Your client must attend the pre-drywall meeting. They will walk through the house at its completed, framed stage, with wall studs, a roof, and all electrical and rough plumbing in place.

During this construction phase, your client can see through all the walls, making it a perfect time to take pictures for future reference. I suggest your client start at the front of the house and go room by room, taking photos of every wall and ceiling. These pictures will come in handy when they want to hang a shelf or install a light fixture and need to know where the studs are located. Additionally, your client can capture the location of plumbing and electrical lines so they don't accidentally drill into them later.

Some volume builders allow adding electrical extras at this phase or changing the location of an electrical outlet or wall switch. Advise your client to check with the on-site salesperson before the pre-drywall meeting on the builder's electrical change policy.

In addition to checking electrical wall and outlet locations, advise your client to verify that all structural changes have been made and are accounted for, and that the builder is aware of all options purchased. Tell them to ask questions if something does not look as expected. Construction supervisors build more than just their home; a good average is twelve to fifteen houses. Sometimes, significant details are overlooked.

For example, an agent in one of my construction classes said their builder should have included an optional French door off the foyer for their client. Because drywall was already in place, the builder refused to correct the mistake. This builder's mistake could have been easily fixed if it had been brought to the supervisor's attention. Builders often miss things; it's not done intentionally, but it happens. That is why attendance at pre-drywall meetings is so vital.

Your client's mindset should be that this is not just a meeting but an inspection.

After completing the walk-through, the supervisor will review the remaining phases of the construction process. Inform your client that they should not expect a closing date. At this phase of construction, there are just too many unknowns.

Changes and Third-Party Inspector

Before moving on to the next builder meeting, I would like you to consider the following two points.

First, your client cannot change the home's design at the drywall stage, even if they are willing to pay a change fee. Stress to your clients the importance of making all selections and upgrades before construction begins.

The second point is to hire a third-party inspector to conduct the Pre-Drywall Inspection if it is not included as a standard feature. Therefore, please check with your builder of choice to determine if they offer this service or if they will allow your client to pay for it and take action on any defects identified by the third party. The average pre-drywall inspection costs between $250 and $500 and takes about two hours to complete.

Please note that I am not suggesting that your client not attend the inspection. I believe their attendance is vital. Having a third-party inspector conduct the review lets your client focus on the inspection, take pictures and notes, and ask questions about any potential uncovered issues.

Your Role

Once again, your role is at the discretion of your client. However, I recommend you talk with your client about where your participation might be welcomed. The first is providing advice, and the second is assisting. The advice is to hire a third-party inspector to conduct the pre-drywall inspection alongside the construction supervisor, and the second is to help during the inspection by taking notes and photographs if not done by your client. Your assistance in taking notes and pictures enables your client to focus on the inspection without worrying about recording what has been heard and seen for future reference.

<u>PRE-CLOSING INSPECTION MEETING</u>

The Pre-Closing Inspection is your client's opportunity to address any construction issues before they sign their closing documents. Many builders call this inspection a *"**Blue Tape Walk-Through**"* because any flaws are marked with blue tape. The builder will also write identified defects on the punch list. If the builder tells your client *"Not to worry"* about an imperfection because it is being addressed, advise them to insist that the issue be added to the punch list. Your client must understand that when a builder says, *"Not to worry,"* it is time for them to start worrying. Tell your client to request a copy of the punch list for their records. The best advice I can offer to share with your clients is to *"**Trust, but Validate**."*

The timing of this meeting is typically scheduled five to seven days before settlement. This allows the builder sufficient time to make necessary repairs. However, some materials and supplies may not be available, making it impossible to complete before closing. Volume builders typically include a clause in the contract that addresses this situation. The contract wording may read: ***"Closing will take place even if some work needs to be completed on the house, provided a Certificate of Occupancy has been issued."***

To prepare your client for this possibility, I recommend that you and your client review the contract before the Pre-Closing Inspection to understand their rights. Advise your client to bring the following with them to the inspection:

- The purchase agreement.

- The home inspection report, if applicable.

- A notebook to record details about any areas of concern.

- A phone or camera to take photos of any problems or damage the builder needs to repair.

- A plug-in tester to verify that the outlets are functioning correctly.

What follows are interior and exterior checklists you can type, print, and give to clients. Please warn them that completing these lists may take several hours and recommend that they take their time with the inspection process. Purchasing a home may be the most significant investment of their lifetime, which calls for a thorough and intensive review. Please remind your clients that, in inclement weather on the inspection day, they should bring rain gear, including boots, umbrellas, and all-weather coats.

Exterior Checklist:

- Does the ground slope away from the house's foundation? The slope should be noticeable and settle over the next several months. However, if it is not visible now, there may be drainage and foundation problems in the future. ☐ **Y** ☐ **N**

- Test sprinkler system. ☐ **Y** ☐ **N**

- Check swells for standing water. ☐ **Y** ☐ **N**

- Inspect fencing for cracked boards and proper nailing. ☐ **Y** ☐ **N**

- Test gates to ensure they are closing correctly. ☐ **Y** ☐ **N**

- Do the gutters and downspouts direct water away from the foundation? ☐ **Y** ☐ **N**

- Shingles are tight and flat, with no signs of buckling. ☐ **Y** ☐ **N**

- All exterior trim is securely fastened. ☐ **Y** ☐ **N**

- All exterior masonry is securely fastened and free from cracks and chips. ☐ **Y** ☐ **N**

- All windows are well caulked around the window frame where the frame meets the house's exterior wall. ☐ **Y** ☐ **N**

- The concrete on the porch and steps is sturdy, with no cracks or gaps. ☐ **Y** ☐ **N**

- The garage door opens and closes completely. ☐ **Y** ☐ **N**

- The light in the garage door opener is working. ☐ **Y** ☐ **N**

- The sensor in the garage door opener is working. Close the garage door and place an object in its path. Ensure the door stops and then fully opens. ☐ **Y** ☐ **N**

- Garage floor and walls are free of cracks, gaps, and other irregularities. ☐ **Y** ☐ **N**

- All exterior electrical outlets are operational and equipped with weather covers. ☐ **Y** ☐ **N**

- All exterior lights are working. ☐ **Y** ☐ **N**

- Doorbell works. ☐ **Y** ☐ **N**

- All post-tension cable locations are filled with concrete. ☐ **Y** ☐ **N**

- Verify that the brick includes weep holes. ☐ **Y** ☐ **N**

- Examine the foundation for cracks or unevenness. ☐ **Y** ☐ **N**

- Confirm with the Construction Supervisor that the termite treatment has been completed. ☐ **Y** ☐ **N**

<u>Interior Checklist</u>:

Doors:

- All doors open and close smoothly and are well-fitted to their frames. There are no gaps where the door meets the floor. ☐ **Y** ☐ **N**

- All door hinges and hardware are clean and free of paint. ☐ **Y** ☐ **N**

- Door knobs are in good working order and are well-fixed to the door. Test all locks to confirm they are working correctly. ☐ **Y** ☐ **N**

- All sides of the door are painted. ☐ **Y** ☐ **N**

- All thresholds are secure and free of gaps between floor types. ☐ **Y** ☐ **N**

- All door trims are secure and well-painted. ☐ **Y** ☐ **N**

- Door stoppers/bumpers are in place, secure, and operate as intended. ☐ **Y** ☐ **N**

- All closet doors open and close easily and are well-fitted with no large gaps. ☐ **Y** ☐ **N**

Windows:

- All windows open and close easily. ☐ **Y** ☐ **N**

- All operable windows lock properly. ☐ **Y** ☐ **N**

- All operable windows have screens, are free of rips, and are secure. ☐ **Y** ☐ **N**

- Window panes are not broken, cracked, or chipped. ☐ **Y** ☐ **N**

- All windows close tightly with a seal. ☐ **Y** ☐ **N**

Floors:

- The carpet is tightly fitted, and the seams are well-matched. ☐ **Y** ☐ **N**

- The carpets are free of stains and discoloration. ☐ **Y** ☐ **N**

- Vinyl and linoleum are free of gaps, scuffs, and scratches, are well-fitted around the edges, and are smooth and bump-free. ☐ **Y** ☐ **N**

- Wood floors are free of chips and cracks, are well-fitted to corners, and are straight. ☐ **Y** ☐ **N**

- Tile grout is well-fitted and free of gaps and chips. ☐ **Y** ☐ **N**

Walls:

- Baseboards are securely fitted, have well-fitting corners, and are free from nail holes and damage. ☐ **Y** ☐ **N**

- Wall paint is even, free of scuffs, marks, and scratches. ☐ **Y** ☐ **N**

- Walls are even, with no signs of drywall blemishes or nail pops. ☐ **Y** ☐ **N**

Kitchen:

- Test all kitchen appliances (oven, range, garbage disposal, refrigerator, microwave, etc.) to ensure they work properly. ☐ **Y** ☐ **N**

- Inspect the kitchen thoroughly. Take photos of blemishes. ☐ **Y** ☐ **N**

- Countertops are free of scratches and scuffs. Check the sides. ☐ **Y** ☐ **N**

- Countertops are level and secure to their base. ☐ **Y** ☐ **N**

- Cabinets are well anchored to the wall. ☐ **Y** ☐ **N**

- All cabinet doors open and close easily, without rubbing or hitting other furnishings. ☐ **Y** ☐ **N**

- All cabinet doors are level, have rubber door steps, and close without a gap. ☐ **Y** ☐ **N**

- All cabinet shelves are level, well-finished, and securely in place. ☐ **Y** ☐ **N**

- Cabinet and drawer handles are securely fastened and free from damage. ☐ **Y** ☐ **N**

- All drawers open easily and do not rub or hit other furnishings. ☐ Y ☐ N

- All drawers close flush and without gaps. ☐ Y ☐ N

- The kitchen faucet has hot and cold water with good water pressure. ☐ Y ☐ N

- The sink is well-caulked around the countertop and is free of chips, damage, and discoloration. ☐ Y ☐ N

- Sink pipes are leak-free, and no water accumulates on the cupboard floor. ☐ Y ☐ N

- The cabinet baseboards are free of damage, well-fitted, and securely in place. ☐ Y ☐ N

- The range hood operates at all speeds, is secure, and the light functions properly. ☐ Y ☐ N

Bathroom:

- Sink and tub are free of scratches, chips, and other damage. ☐ Y ☐ N

- Sink and tub hold water. ☐ Y ☐ N

- Run water to ensure all plumbing systems drain thoroughly. ☐ Y ☐ N

- Sink and tub fixtures are securely installed, providing hot and cold water. ☐ Y ☐ N

- Sink and tub are well caulked. ☐ **Y** ☐ **N**

- The toilet is secure to the floor. ☐ **Y** ☐ **N**

- The toilet paper dispenser is at a good distance and height from the toilet. ☐ **Y** ☐ **N**

- Countertops and drawers are free of scratches, chips, and other damage. ☐ **Y** ☐ **N**

- Cabinets and drawers are free of damage and open and close properly. ☐ **Y** ☐ **N**

- Back-splash is well-fitted and caulked. ☐ **Y** ☐ **N**

- Toilet flushes properly. It doesn't run for too long. ☐ **Y** ☐ **N**

- Shower tiles are secure with no gaps and well-sealed grout. ☐ **Y** ☐ **N**

- Bathroom fans work. ☐ **Y** ☐ **N**

Heating & A/C:

- Confirm that the heating, ventilation, and air conditioning system is fully functional. ☐ **Y** ☐ **N**

- Vents are not located under thermostat sensors and are clear of debris. ☐ **Y** ☐ **N**

- Air return vents are unobstructed. ☐ **Y** ☐ **N**

- Gas fireplace (if applicable) works. ☐ **Y** ☐ **N**

Electrical:

- All interior electrical outlets are working. ☐ **Y** ☐ **N**

- All light switches work as intended. ☐ **Y** ☐ **N**

- Turn on ceiling fans to ensure they are working correctly. ☐ **Y** ☐ **N**

- The breaker switches in the electrical breaker panel are clearly labeled. ☐ **Y** ☐ **N**

- Confirm all the overhead lights work by turning them on and off. ☐ **Y** ☐ **N**

- Test all smoke detectors. ☐ **Y** ☐ **N**

Plumbing:

- The water heater is the size included on the standard feature sheet. ☐ **Y** ☐ **N**

Miscellaneous:

- Verify that all options and structural options are included and accounted for. ☐ **Y** ☐ **N**

When the interior and exterior checklists are combined, it becomes clear that the inspection may be more than your clients can handle. Because of this, please advise your client to hire an independent third-party inspector with knowledge and expertise in new home construction. This is a decision that they will not regret. Yes, there is a cost, and your client must get permission from the builder.

I will discuss this suggestion further and add details in Chapter Nine, Volume Builder Services.

Your Role

As I stated, your client has the final say on whether or not you attend builder meetings. The Pre-Closing Inspection is no exception; however, I recommend attending it because of its importance. Your client's emotions are running high; the closing is within sight, and they naturally worry that if they find too many construction flaws, it might delay or postpone the settlement. Because you are not emotionally involved, you are well-positioned to advocate for your client. Your presence at the Pre-Closing Inspection ensures that their voice is heard. This is why builders prefer home buyers to attend the inspection without their Realtor.

I do not suggest you take over the inspection. It is between your client and the construction supervisor. The interior and exterior checklists serve as reminders of what requires inspection. Your role is to confirm that every item on the checklist is reviewed. Your clients have the final say on what will be repaired, replaced, or left as-is.

PRE-CLOSING ORIENTATION MEETING

The Pre-Closing Orientation Meeting is your client's final walkthrough before closing and moving into their new home. Typically, the construction supervisor conducts the orientation; however, the on-site salesperson may lead it, or, if the volume builder is large enough, a Customer Care Manager. Generally, the orientation lasts between one to two hours. Your attendance at this meeting is not necessary.

Most Pre-Closing Orientations include the following four steps:

- Review the punch list to verify that all items listed for repair or replacement have been completed to the client's satisfaction.

- Home walkthrough.

- Basic maintenance tutorials.

- Warranty discussion.

These steps may differ slightly from builder to builder, but every volume builder's walkthrough checklist includes the items listed above.

Punch List Review

During the punch list review, the construction supervisor will show your client the repair or replacement of each item listed. If your client is satisfied with the repair or replacement, they will be asked to initial their approval. If not, the item remains on the list until the client is satisfied. If the home has received a Certificate of Occupancy, the repair or replacement will be completed after closing. Remind your client to request a copy of the revised punch list.

Home Walk-Through

In the next step, the construction supervisor will conduct a walk-through of the home. This means explaining essential operational information related to utilities:

- The location of the breaker box and how to identify which break-ers control which electrical outlets. ☐ **Y** ☐ **N**

- Location of the main electrical shut-off. ☐ **Y** ☐ **N**

- The location of shut-off devices to gas or propane lines. ☐ **Y** ☐ **N**

- Location of the main water line and its shut-off valve. ☐ **Y** ☐ **N**

Other walkthrough items your client can expect include:

- Introduction to appliances, including oven, microwave, refrigerator, dishwasher, and garbage disposal. A brief review of appliance warranties and the importance of registering products with the manufacturer. ☐ **Y** ☐ **N**

- Tips about energy efficiency, including doors, windows, attic insulation, and how to prevent pipes from freezing over the winter. ☐ **Y** ☐ **N**

- How to operate the exterior and interior door locks and the location of door keys. ☐ **Y** ☐ **N**

- How smoke and carbon monoxide detectors operate, battery or direct wiring. Warning: If detectors are disabled, home warranty coverage may be affected. ☐ **Y** ☐ **N**

After the walkthrough, the construction supervisor will discuss common maintenance tips with your client. They are:

- How to operate and program the thermostat. ☐ **Y** ☐ **N**

- How to change the HVAC air filters. ☐ **Y** ☐ **N**

- How to operate the irrigation system. ☐ **Y** ☐ **N**

- How to set alarm codes (if applicable). ☐ Y ☐ N

- How to set the garage door remote and sensors (if applicable). ☐ Y ☐ N

- How to drain and maintain the water heater. ☐ Y ☐ N

- How to test and reset the house's GFCI receptacles. ☐ Y ☐ N

- How to maintain the house's foundation. ☐ Y ☐ N

Lastly, the construction supervisor will discuss the builder's home warranty:

- The client will learn about warranty information associated with the home. ☐ Y ☐ N

- How long the warranty coverage lasts. ☐ Y ☐ N

- How to submit warranty requests. ☐ Y ☐ N

The builder will discuss what constitutes an urgent request and how to contact the appropriate vendor if the warranty request is urgent and needs to be handled promptly. An example is a plumbing or gas leak, or HVAC failure.

I will discuss warranties further and add details in Chapter Nine, Volume Builder Services.

Your Role

As I stated, attending the Pre-Closing Orientation is unnecessary if you participated in the other three builder and homebuyer meetings, where you offered advice, opinions, took notes, and pictures. Because you partic-ipated in the other builder meetings, your client is ready for the last builder meeting without your assistance.

However, I do suggest meeting with your client the day before the Pre-Closing Orientation and reviewing with them what to expect during the orientation. Please start with the four orientation steps, followed by a review of what to expect regarding the punch list, what home products will be reviewed during the home walk-through, and a discussion of common maintenance tips by the construction supervisor to ensure the products within the home function properly for years to come. Finally, a review of the home warranties, what constitutes an urgent service request, and how to contact the appropriate vendor.

Furthermore, I suggest you give them a copy of the Hhome Walkthrough Checklists. With this printed information, your client will have all they need to participate in the final builder before closing without concern or worry.

With that said, if your client wants you to attend, please do. Your role is to manage the home walkthrough lists and to be the note and picture taker.

Chapter Eight Key Takeaways

Chapter Eight provides an overview of the key aspects you need to know about possible construction meetings between your client and the home builder. To reinforce your understanding of the material in this chapter, take a few minutes to answer the following three questions? Answering these key takeaways will strengthen your understanding of the chapter's main ideas and aid your ongoing learning about working and partnering with the new home builder community.

1. What spoke to you most about this chapter?

2. What insight in these pages made the most significant impression on you?

3. How will you take what you have learned in this chapter, and put it into action in your pursuit of new home sales?

Volume Builder Services

V OLUME BUILDERS PROVIDE UP to three valuable home buyer services; they are:

- Third-Party Inspection?

- Third-Party Warranty.

- After-Closing Service Program.

I placed a question mark behind Third-Party Inspection because there are differences in how volume builders handle construction reviews by an outside entity. Some production builders welcome the service and budget the inspections as a cost of doing business. The inspector has access to the house during construction and after construction is complete, and provides the builder with a written report on issues discovered during their reviews.

Other volume builders allow third-party inspectors access to the house after construction, but the home buyer pays for the service. The inspector's written report is provided to the home buyer, who, in turn, gives it to the builder's on-site salesperson, who then provides the report to the construction supervisor. The builder is under no written obligation to act on any construction issues discovered during the review. However, most construction supervisors appreciate learning about possible problems so the issues can be resolved before closing.

Some production builders do not allow third-party inspectors access to the house. This attitude toward third-party inspections is rare, but it does happen.

Third-Party Home Inspection

Now, let's examine what a third-party home inspection is and, more importantly, how it can help your client.

A third-party home inspection is similar to a review of an existing home. Your client can expect the following inspections:

- Foundation.

- Grading.

- House structure.

- Walls, ceilings, and floors.

- Windows and doors.

- Roof.

- Attic.

- Insulation.

- HVAC system.

- Plumbing.

- Electrical.

When an inspector comes to the house, they spend two to four hours checking the abovementioned areas for problems. They take notes, measurements, and pictures and combine the information into a formal report that the builder or client (depending on who paid for the service) receives soon after the home inspection is completed.

How Does a Third-Party Inspector Benefit Your Client

Although local county or city inspectors examine the house during construction and builders check the quality of subcontractors' work, some problem areas might be overlooked during those reviews. Third-party inspectors are impartial and have no stake in the inspection's outcome, which ensures that the inspection is fair and unbiased. Therefore, a third-party inspection can help your client avoid significant repairs by identifying potential construction defects before your client takes ownership.

Here are the benefits of third-party inspection:

- Peace of Mind.

- Protect your client's investment.

- Avoid unexpected expenses.

Client Participation During Third-Party Inspection?

Usually, a home inspector will not mind if your client is present during the inspection unless they interfere with it. Most inspectors might even encourage your client to attend so that they can point out specific issues and concerns in real-time and answer questions about whether defects should be replaced, repaired, or left as-is.

How Much Does a Third-Party Inspection Cost?

According to estimates from the US Department of Housing and Urban Development, a third-party home inspection for a single-family home can cost between $300 and $500. The actual price will depend on the house's size, the inspection's scale, and price increases due to inflation.

Minimum Requirements for a Third-Party Inspector

When hiring a third-party home inspector, the minimum requirement your client should look for is their license. Additionally, your client should look for any certifications the home inspector has earned. A certification is a positive sign that the inspector is experienced and has the knowledge to perform a complete and accurate home inspection. Have your client look for the following certifications:

- The American Society of Home Inspectors (ASHI).

- The National Association of Home Inspectors (NAHI).

- The International Association of Certified Home Inspectors (InterNACHI).

Your Role

Your client has a choice: they can inspect the house for problems during the Pre-Closing Meeting or hire a third-party inspector. The decision should be based on the time available to perform a thorough inspection, their knowledge of construction, and the funds available to pay the inspector.

Your role is to help your client make an informed decision. Ask your client the following two questions:

1. A thorough new home examination will take two to three hours. Do you have the time to do a comprehensive new home inspection?

2. A new home inspection requires construction knowledge. Do you have the construction expertise necessary for an extensive new home inspection?

If your client answers the first question affirmatively, copy, print, and distribute the Interior and Exterior Home Checklists included in the Pre-Closing Inspection. If you have time, you may consider offering your assistance.

To further support your client, recommend they go to YouTube and search new home inspections or new home inspector. There, your client will find short and long videos to help them understand how to conduct a thorough house exam. If your client answers the second question in the negative, then assist your client in finding a third-party new home inspector. Tell them to begin their search by Googling "*New Home Inspector Near Me*."

If your client wants to hire a third-party inspector but needs more funds, consider gifting them the inspection cost. This is a gift they will appreciate and remember when asked to refer you to their family and friends.

THIRD-PARTY WARRANTY

It is not if something will go wrong with your client's new home; it is when it will go wrong. To give your client peace of mind, most volume builders, but not all, provide a third-party warranty that protects home buyers from labor and material defects and structural problems found after construction is complete. What follows is what your client can expect from a third-party warranty.

Third-Party Warranty Coverage

Materials and labor (1 year)

- Non-Load-Bearing Walls

- Paint or Stains

- Drywall

- Flooring

- Doors, Trim, Cabinets, Hardware, Insulation,

- Windows

- Exterior Siding

* Landscaping Materials

* Light Fixtures

House Mechanicals (2 Years)

* HVAC Systems

* Ductwork

* Plumbing

* Electrical Work

Major Structural Defects (Up to 10 Years)

* Footings and Foundation Systems

* Beams

* Columns

* Load-Bearing Walls

* Roof Framing Systems

* Floor Framing Systems

* Masonry Arches

Third-Party Warranty Exceptions

The third-party warranty does not cover damage caused by normal wear and tear, weather, additions made to the house, or homeowner negligence.

Third-party warranties do not cover household appliances, so if your client has problems with an appliance, they must contact the manufacturer directly.

At the Pre-Closing Orientation, the construction supervisor will provide your client with all the warranties included in any manufactured product used in the construction of the house. Please advise your client to register the warranty for each manufactured product.

Also, some third-party warranties are not transferable to the buyer if your client decides to sell their home within the warranty period. Advise your client to ask the on-site salesperson or the construction supervisor if the third-party warranty is transferable.

Third-Party Warranty Questions

When you and your client choose a builder, enquiring about the type of Third-Party Warranty included with the home purchase is essential because they are not all the same. Some questions to ask:

- **<u>What does the warranty cover?</u>** Third-party warranties typically cover structure elements, home systems, foundations, roofs, framing, walls, floors, ceilings, doors, windows, and quality. Advise your client to read the warranty, not just scan it.

- **<u>What is the warranty's timeline?</u>** Ensure your client understands what parts of the home are covered and for how long. Remember, material and labor are covered differently from structural elements.

- **<u>What are the exclusions?</u>** Every third-party warranty will have exclusions, so advise your client to read the fine print. Standard exclusions include damage caused by normal wear and tear or weather-related damage.

- **<u>Is there a deductible?</u>** While uncommon, some third-party warranties will have a deductible, the amount your client must pay out of pocket before the policy kicks in. Deductibles can range from five hundred to two thousand dollars, so advise your client to check the policy before signing an agreement.

Third-Party Warranty Performance Standards

The following two examples help you understand the performance standards your client will likely encounter in their third-party warranty.

Possible Deficiency: Ground settling around foundation, utility trenches, or other filled areas.

Performance Standard: If the builder established the final grading, it would fill areas that have settled more than five inches once at the end of the Warranty Period. The Owner will remove and replace any landscaping required to perform corrective work.

***

Possible Deficiency: Erosion and washed-out areas.

Performance Standard: Unless noted on the buyer's walkthrough punch list, the Owner must maintain adequate ground cover to prevent erosion. Therefore, it is expressly excluded from this warranty.

The third-party warranty includes a wide array of performance standards, so there is no mistake about who is responsible for what. Your client must read the policy and place it where it can be quickly found. Remember this fact: ***"It is not if something will go wrong with your client's new home; it is when it will go wrong."***

Your Role

When your client decides to buy a newly constructed home, a third-party warranty protects against unforeseen problems that threaten the very foundation of their investment. You must ensure your client understands the type of warranty the builder provides.

Some volume builders, due to their size and financial strength, self-insure. The downside to a builder who self-insures is going out of business. If the builder is gone, so are the warranties. One way your clients can protect themselves if a builder self-insures is to purchase a supplemental structural warranty from a third party. To learn more about third-party warranty costs, your client can use their favorite search engine and type: *Structural New Home Warranty Cost.*

Other volume builders include a third-party warranty as a standard feature, transferring the risk to an insurance-backed company. With a Third-Party Warranty, your client is protected with or without the builder.

Once your client understands what type of warranty comes with the home purchase, they must understand the following:

- **Exclusions**: Warranty exclusions are typically outlined in a separate section of the warranty document.

- **Transferable**: Ensure your client confirms that the builder's warranty is transferable to subsequent homeowners if they must sell the property before it expires.

- **Deductibles**: Confirm there are no deductibles when making a claim.

- **Manufacturers' Warranties**: Advise your client to complete every manufacturer's warranty and send it so the product is registered with the manufacturer.

AFTER-CLOSING SERVICE

Your client completed a walkthrough with the construction supervisor the week before closing and generated a punch list of items that need attention. Many items on that list were repaired or replaced during the week leading up to the closing, but some remain in progress. So, what is the proper protocol to handle incomplete punch list items and after-closing service requests?

First Post-Sale Year

Most volume builders have a specific service program for the first year after closing that allows callback requests. The program typically includes your client's Construction Supervisor and the Builder's Warranty Department.

The construction supervisor is accountable for unfinished items on the punch list created at the Pre-Closing Inspection, and the Warranty Department takes responsibility for the house after the home buyer acknowledges that items on the punch list have been repaired or replaced to their satisfaction.

The following will help your client understand the After-Closing Service Program and provide them with some best practices to follow.

Builder Documents

In most volume builder situations, your client received the following four documents that cover how the builder will manage punch lists and service requests. They are:

1. Builder Contract and Addenda.

2. Limited Warranty.

3. Home Owner's Guide.

4. Manufacturer Warranties.

These documents outline the following:

- How to communicate regarding a warranty claim or repair issue.

- The entity responsible for each type of repair.

- Length of coverage for repairs or replacements.

Remind your clients that before they contact the Warranty Department for a service request, they should review the appropriate document to understand their rights and the builder's responsibility for the service issue. Additionally, tell your client to store these documents in a safe location that allows them quick access.

Pre-Close Inspection Punch List

Most volume builders will acknowledge that their homes will not be one hundred percent complete on the day of closing. They add a clause to the purchase agreement that covers punch list items to protect themselves. What follows was taken from one volume builder's contract, however, what follows may be different for other volume builders, but the items covered in the following will be similar for all volume builders. The paragraph reads as such:

*"**Within a reasonable period** following the closing, Seller shall remedy the punch list items and make adjustments as agreed to by Buyer and Seller in a walk-through inspection scheduled by Seller and Buyer before closing.*

*The seller and seller's agent shall be **provided full access to the property** to remedy the punch list items. The existence of such punch list items or other nonstructural imperfections shall not entitle the Buyer to cancel this contract, withhold funds at the closing, or delay the closing.*

*After closing, the seller shall have **no further or continuing responsibility for periodic inspection**, replacement, maintenance, or repair of improvements except for punch list items identified before the closing in writing or as may be covered **by the Limited Warranty."***

Your client must fully understand the four points underlined in the above paragraphs. When they know what actions will be taken to correct defects, your client can work with, not against, the builder. By adopting this mindset, problems get fixed promptly, and your client can get on with their lives.

The following examines each underlined point:

- **<u>Within a reasonable period</u>**: Remind your client to ask the construction supervisor at the Pre-Closing Orientation what constitutes a reasonable period to complete the list of unfinished punch list items. For most volume builders, a reasonable amount of time is thirty days.

- **<u>Provide full access to the property</u>**: Ask your client to speak with the builder for clarification on what is meant by full access. If both of your clients work, this could become troublesome. My only warning is that if your client does not make their home available for repair when scheduled, they risk the repair not being completed within a reasonable period.

- **<u>No further or continuing responsibility for periodic inspections</u>**: Tell your client to discuss the sentence's meaning with the on-site salesperson during the contract review. Does it mean there are no other scheduled inspections to repair defects that appear after the punch list items are completed? If the answer they receive is "*Yes*," then remind your client of the importance of the Pre-Closing Inspection.

- **<u>Limited warranty</u>**: Remind your client to ask the construction supervisor when the Limited Warranty begins. Is it the day of closing or when punch list items are completed?

Limited Warranty

For a builder's After-Close Service to operate efficiently, tell your client to wait at least sixty days after closing before submitting warranty lists. This allows them adequate time to live with the products included in the construction of their home. If your client feels a part of their new home is damaged due to a construction defect, and it is affecting the house's livability, advise them to report it to the Warranty Department immediately.

Warranty repairs are generally scheduled for repair within thirty days of receipt of your client's written request. However, remind your client that circumstances beyond the builder's control may cause a delay in repair or replacement. Delays may be caused by shortages of materials, back-ordered parts, labor problems, weather, and scheduling conflicts.

11th Month Punch List

No other periodic inspections are scheduled after the completion of the Pre-Inspection Punch List. From that time forward, the homeowner will be responsible for the care and maintenance of the home. However, most volume builders will accept a request for service before the builder's one-year warranty expires.

Advise your client to begin a list of items they feel are the builder's responsibility. Instruct them to be thorough when developing their list, and take a picture with a time stamp if necessary. This is your client's last opportunity to correct non-structural construction defects. Mail the list and photos to the builder in the care of the Warranty Department. The mailing address can be found in the Home Owner's Guide your client receives during the Pre-Closing Orientation Meeting.

When the builder receives your client's request for service, they will decide whether the item is covered under the warranty or if it is the homeowner's responsibility. Following review, your client will receive a phone call or email alerting them to the action for each item listed on the request for service form.

Emergency Services

Advise your client to report an emergency quickly. The builder is not responsible for any subsequent damage caused by a delay in reporting an emergency. Additionally, the builder's Limited Warranty does not cover damage to personal property.

What follows are considered emergencies by most volume builders:

- Total loss of heating or air conditioning during extreme weather conditions.

- Total loss of electricity. Check with the utility company before contacting the builder.

- Plumbing leak that requires the entire water supply to the home to be shut off.

- Gas leak. If the leak is in the furnace or water heater supply lines, contact your utility company or a plumber.

- Electrical problem that is a fire hazard or a source of danger.

- A total stoppage of the plumbing drain system. Example: The main sewer line is clogged, making it impossible to utilize the plumbing system.

- Any other problem that, without immediate correction and preventive measures, creates a potential for bodily harm that cannot be reasonably avoided.

Your Role

Your role in the After-Close Service is limited to advice. Your client, not you, must handle any issues with the house. However, you can provide some best practices for communicating with the builder regarding construction defects.

I strongly recommend emailing your client the following methods to track communications. This will mitigate future confusion on service requests and provide security and organization in your dealings.

Best Practices:

- Make notes on every conversation with the builder.

- Track the time and date of conversations, communications (written or verbal), and contacts (phone, email, text, or in-person).

- Take and keep copies of pictures of any problem areas.

- Keep all original builder correspondence.

- Follow up with a phone call to ensure your service request was received.

- Retain copies of all correspondence sent from the builder.

Effective client communication is critical in the real estate business. By promptly addressing concerns with the builder and avoiding outside agencies, your client can ensure a smooth process and will allow them to feel heard and valued.

Builders, like you, depend on referrals. They want your clients to be happy and share their experiences with family and friends. If your clients have problems with service requests, remind them of this advice: **"You can catch more flies with honey than with vinegar."** This saying underscores the power of kindness and politeness in persuasion, a principle that can foster better client relationships.

CHAPTER NINE KEY TAKEAWAYS

Chapter Nine provides an overview of the key aspects you need to know about possible services a volume home builder provides before, during, and after construction is completed. To reinforce your understanding of the material in this chapter, take a few minutes to answer the following three questions? Answering these key takeaways will strengthen your understanding of the chapter's main ideas and aid your ongoing learning about working and partnering with the new home builder community.

1.   What spoke to you most about this chapter?

2.   What insight in these pages made the most significant impression on you?

3.   How will you take what you have learned in this chapter, and put it into action in your pursuit of new home sales?

Researching Volume Builders

Earlier, I identified four builder types and explained how best to work with each one. As a reminder, here are the different builder types I named:

1. Multi-Family Home Builder.

2. Custom Home Builder.

3. Semi-Custom Home Builder.

4. Volume Home Builder.

I strongly recommend focusing your real estate new home sales strategy on volume home builders. This choice offers numerous benefits and aligns with most production builders' services, giving you a solid foundation to assist your clients in finding the right home in the right location and at the right price.

YOUR TASK in this chapter is to identify one volume builder that will satisfy the majority of your future new home clients. I limited the number to **_one volume builder_** because I want you to feel that what you are asked to do is manageable.

If you recall, in the Introduction of this book, I wrote that you will be asked to perform tasks. Over the following four chapters, you will be asked to complete many tasks. When you complete a task, you will have learned something that will demonstrate your difference to a builder and, more importantly, it will set you up for new home sales success. Please take your time with each task. If you don't understand the task, go back and reread the chapter until you comprehend what you are being asked to do. The tasks are not complex, but they will take time. Be patient, be alert, and be aware. Everything you need to know about a volume builder is right in front of you if you know what to look and listen for.

Your first task begins with research. Let's get started.

IDENTIFYING A VOLUME BUILDER PARTNER

Researching the right builder and community for you and your clients has three parts, they are:

- Identifying the right volume builder partner for you and your clients.

- Finding a community that your selected volume builder serves.

- Finalizing your volume builder choice.

What follows are the six steps to identify a volume builder partner:

- Compiling a list of national and local volume builders in your market area.

- Reviewing their websites.

- Finding and reading their online reviews.

- Selecting a volume builder and community to tour.

- Confirm your volume builder and community choices with your agent peers.

- Starting.

National, Regional, or Local Volume Builder List

Finding the right volume home builder partner for you and your clients begins with you opening a Word document on your computer and starting a list of volume home builders that come to mind. The list you compile may only include a few builders, which is okay. Don't worry; the number of builders listed is not critical. I want you to stop, save, and close the document. It would be best if you did nothing else about compiling your list until your next real estate office meeting.

Talk With Your Broker

Before your next office meeting, call your broker and tell them you want to add new home sales to your business plan. Ask for permission to address the agents. Your broker may ask you some questions, so be prepared to discuss your new home sales objectives and the strategies you intend to utilize to accomplish your goals.

At the meeting, tell the agents what you are doing about adding new homes to your business strategy and that you need their help. In my experience, people want to help; all you have to do is ask. Consider the following request for assistance:

***

I aim to add new home sales to my real estate business strategy. My focus will be on volume home builders. The qualities I am looking for in a builder are reputation, homeowner satisfaction, a variety of house designs, a builder with a mortgage and a title company option, good construction quality, excellent resale value, communication before, during, and after the sale, and a builder with an impressive list of standard features and upgrades, and last, but certainly, not least, problem-solving because there has not been a house built that didn't have some issues that need to be resolved. Here is where I need your help. What builders are you comfortable referring to your clients?

***

When you approach the agents, it's crucial to emphasize that you're not just asking for builders who meet specific criteria but for builders they trust and would be comfortable referring to their clients. This distinction will help them understand their significant role in your strategy.

Follow Up with Agents

Additionally, ask your broker for permission to follow up with the agents who attended the meeting. When you get permission from your broker, tell the agents you will send them a follow-up email and that you would appreciate a reply or, better yet, a phone call. Here is an email you might send:

***

Hi, it is (insert your name). I appreciate you listening to my request for help at this morning's sales meeting. Your recommendations for volume home builders are highly valued as I seek to enhance my real estate business strategy. Providing a list of builders you have either introduced to your clients or would feel comfortable recommending would be incredibly beneficial. I look forward to hearing from you soon with your recommendations. If you have any questions, I am available at your convenience. Your insights are crucial to my decision-making. I would appreciate a prompt response.

***

Finally, I want to stress the value of word-of-mouth recommendations in the search for a volume builder. Personal experiences from friends, family, and acquaintances who have recently purchased homes can provide invaluable insights into the quality of work a builder offers and whether they would be a good fit for your business strategy.

Separate National Volume Builders From Regional and Local Volume Builders

When you receive a builder's name, add it to your list. You will likely have compiled an impressive list of volume home builders. Next, separate the builders into national, regional, and local builders. The reason for the separation is that through your research, you will find differences when you compare them. The differences you will find in builder benefits and services may be slight, but those differences will be what causes you to refer one builder over another. Understanding the differences between builders gives you credibility; the more credible you are, the more people will want to work with you.

Add Builder Folders to Bookmark Bar

This next step will take several hours to complete. You will set up folders and subfolders on your favorite search engine for the builders you and others have recommended. I will use my favorite search engine, Google, to explain the process step-by-step. Once I have opened Google, I go to the Bookmark Bar, right-click, and select Add Folder from the Drop-Down Menu. I named the new folder National Production Builders, clicked the Bookmark Bar, and saved it. I do the same thing for Regional and Local Production Builders.

My Bookmark Bar now has a National, Regional, and Local Production Builders Folder. If they are not visible, locate the arrow on the Bookmark Bar and click on it. I now see all the folders or URLs that have been saved. I drag both folders to my Bookmark Bar's front for quick access.

Add Builder Names to Folders

Next, I need to move the builders I selected for this exercise into the three folders I created. To do this, I browse for one of the builders on my list. For example, I have chosen Lennar Homes, a National Volume Builder. Once Lennar's home page is open, I click the Star on the right side of the Bookmark Bar. This action opens the Edit Bookmark tab, and I enter

Lennar's name; then I click the down arrow, select National Production Builder Folder, and click Done.

Lennar Homes will be visible when I click National Production Builder on the Bookmark Bar. Next, I browse for every builder on my list and sort them into a National, Regional, or Local Production Builder Folder on my Bookmark Bar.

Ask for Help

If you need assistance in completing this step, ask for it. Don't be embarrassed to ask for help. As you build your new home sales business, I promise you will return to your selected builders frequently for community and product research and to learn what changes, additions, and deletions builders have made to their websites. Builders' websites are updated nightly, and changes can include new information about special promotions, price changes, and quick move-in opportunities. A Builder's Folder allows you to obtain that information quickly.

REVIEW BUILDER WEBSITES

Now that you have set up your Builder Folders, it is time to review each selected builder's website. Typically, you will find information about their homes and communities, their complete and move-in-ready homes, what makes them different from other builders, and how to contact them if you are a homeowner, prospective homebuyer, or Realtor. You will also have access to a chat line for inquiries and, if needed, a place to make a warranty request. The Internet Salesperson monitors the chat line, and warranty requests are directed to the Warranty Department.

As you review each builder's website, look for the following nine qualities that distinguish one builder from another. If something you read or notice stands out, make a note to follow up with the builder's on-site salesperson. Remember, you are looking for differences between builders.

1. Reputation.

2. Homeowner satisfaction.

3. Mortgage and title company option.

4. Variety of home designs.

5. Quality construction.

6. Resale value.

7. Communication before, during, and after the sale.

8. Features and upgrades.

9. Problem-solving.

Finding and Reading Volume Builder Online Reviews

It is time to seriously examine how home buyers who bought from your selected builders feel about their purchase. But before you begin assessing, please consider what the Federal Trade Commission advises on evaluating online reviews.

***

"When you use online reviews to help you make decisions, consider the source(s) of information, what you know about the reviewer (home builder, influencer, or homeowner), and how much confidence you have in the site where you read the review."

***

The FTC's main recommendation is to look at various sources, including well-known websites with trustworthy and impartial expert reviews. That is still a perfect place to start. Here are some other steps to take:

- Check how recent the reviews are; watch for a burst of reviews over a short period. That can sometimes mean the reviews are fake.

- Check if the reviewer has written other reviews. If so, read those to understand better how much to trust that reviewer. If it seems that the reviewer has created an account to write a review for a product, that reviewer might be a paid influencer.

- Don't assume that, just by looking, you can spot the difference between an honest review and a fake one. Some reviews may look suspicious, and some may look real, but it can often be nearly impossible to tell. For example, you already know to watch out for reviews that seem too optimistic to be accurate. Still, some fake positive reviews give less than the highest possible rating to seem more believable.

- Remember that reviews are not always positive. Sometimes, a company might post fake negative reviews to harm a competitor.

You won't always know if a reviewer got something, like a free product, in exchange for writing a review. But, on some websites, you will see a label or badge next to the review telling the reviewer got an incentive. How you weigh those reviews is up to you.

Finding Reliable Sources for Volume Builder Reviews

Finding reliable builder review sources requires time and effort, so most agents skip this step. I suggest you begin with the online platforms specifically designed for this purpose, such as Trust Builder, Life Story Research, Trust Pilot, Houzz, Home Advisor, and Agni, all of which feature home builder reviews.

I recommend starting with Trust Builder: Honest Reviews from Real Home Owners. This site has the most extensive ratings and reviews for home builders nationwide. It is also the only independent source of reviews from verified homeowners. My other recommendation is Life Story Research. They provide a ranking for the most trusted home builders nationwide.

Furthermore, consider checking with the Better Business Bureau (BBB) and Consumer Affairs for any complaints or issues associated with the builder.

Social media platforms like Facebook can also be valuable. They may have groups or pages related to home building or new homes in your area, where you can find real-time reviews and discussions. Lastly, consider going to YouTube and searching for your builder of choice.

Take Detailed Notes for Comparison

When assessing prospective builder reviews online, it is vital to discern between genuine and potentially biased or fraudulent reviews. Try to focus on reviews that provide detailed, specific information about the home-owner's experience rather than simply stating that the service was excellent or terrible without further explanation. The more specific a review is, the more likely it is to provide helpful information.

Don't overlook the review trend. A home builder might have a mix of positive and negative reviews, which is normal. However, noticing a trend of many recent negative reviews might indicate a decline in performance or service level. Similarly, if the builder has consistently received negative feedback over a long period, it is a strong indicator of their reliability and quality of work.

Finally, please note how the builder responds to their reviews, which can provide insight into their customer service approach. A builder who responds professionally and constructively to negative reviews, taking responsibility for any mistakes and offering solutions, shows a company that values home buyers and is committed to quality service.

Take comprehensive notes as you review each builder. If you skip note-taking, you risk forgetting what was said or written, positively or negatively, reducing your ability to compare one builder to another.

Spotting Red Flags in Volume Builder Reviews

When examining reviews, it is crucial to be aware of potential red flags indicating less-than-satisfactory service. What follows are some typical issues to be on the lookout for:

- Poor communication with homeowners.

- Missed deadlines during the construction process.

- Lack of attention to finishing details.

- Cost overruns.

- Unwillingness or delay in returning to fix after-closing defects.

Building a house is a significant investment, and helping your clients make a well-informed decision by referring them to a trustworthy builder will ensure that their investment will stand the test of time. By doing the research, you are setting yourself and your client up for success.

Word of Mouth Reviews

You have done the research, but have yet to find any reviews that provide insight into several of the builders you selected. Don't worry; that is normal. When that happens, you must seek word-of-mouth reviews from people who purchased a home from those builders. From these home-buyers, you can inquire about their sales encounters, the quality of work provided by the builder, ease of communication from sale to closing, the after-sale service they received, and whether they would recommend them or purchase a home from them again. These real-life experiences will be the guide that helps you make an informed decision about whether you should continue researching those builders or remove them from your list.

MORE TO LEARN

Stop reading and give yourself a pat on the back. If you compiled a list of national, regional, and local volume builders in your market area, bookmarked those builders on your favorite search engine, reviewed the websites of your selected builders, and read online reviews for each builder, you have been very busy and have learned a lot. You are to be congratulated because you are well on your way to adding new home sales to your real estate business strategy. However, there is more to learn before you can reap the benefits of all your efforts.

Six Critical Home Buying Decisions

Prospective home buyers make six critical decisions when purchasing a new home, they are:

- Home.

- Homesite.

- Community.

- Location.

- Financing.

- Builder.

In the third book of this series, "*Have You Considered the Possibility of a New Home*," I will discuss each decision-making category in depth. In the meantime, I want to draw your attention to the community and builder because they represent two of the six home-buying decisions.

What you do when selecting a community and builder is similar to what a home buyer does when they choose. Both of you have conditions that must exist before you accept the community and builder as a possibility.

What Qualities Agents and Buyers Want in a Builder

What follows is a list of *"wants"* home buyers and agents typically expect from a builder:

- Solid financial reputation.

- Good quality reputation.

- Variety of home designs.

- Option and structural change availability.

- Third-party warranty.

- Third-party inspection.

- Builder-owned or preferred mortgage and title company.

- After-closing service program.

- Competitive pricing.

YOUR TASK is to determine which builder on your list satisfies the wants of your future homebuyers. Please note that I said builder in the singular. I want you to eliminate every builder on your list but one. For this exercise, I recommend that you select a national volume builder.

It is only fair to warn you before you start this exercise that additional research may be necessary. I have listed thirty questions on the following pages to help you determine if more research is required. Work through them quickly. If you don't have an answer, move to the next question. Remember that this exercise aims to select one builder to visit. The answers you don't have can be learned by additional research or when you meet with the builder's on-site salesperson during your first or second visit, by revisiting the builder's website, or by rereading reviews.

What follows are questions you can ask yourself about the builders on your list.

Solid Financial Reputation:

- How long has the builder been in business?

- Does the builder use lines of credit to build homes or ask the home buyer to take out a construction loan?

- What is their earnest money policy?

- What is their cancellation policy?

Good Quality Construction:

- Based on builder reviews, what word would best describe each builder?

- What is the builder's Better Business Bureau rating?

- Does the builder have a warranty request form on their website?

- Are there any customer endorsement videos or written testimonials online?

Variety of House Designs:

- How many different exterior elevations does the builder offer? (Example: brick and siding, brick, stone, and siding, brick and stucco, etc.)

- How many different roof pitches does the builder offer? (Example: gable, mansard, hip, pyramid, flat, etc.)

- Does the builder offer more than one house design in the community? (Example: single-family detached, townhomes, condos, zero lot line, etc.)

- Are the home designs for first-time, move-up, or downsizing buyers?

Option and Structural Change Availability:

- Are options selections made at the model home or a design center?

- Does the builder offer a large variety of options?

- What structural options are available for purchase?

Third-Party Warranty:

- Does the builder offer a third-party warranty, or are they self-insured?

- How many years is the third-party warranty in effect?

- What does the warranty cover in years one, two, and three through ten?

Third-Party Quality Inspection:

- Does the builder budget for a third-party inspector?

- If the builder does not budget for a third-party inspector, do they allow the client to hire one? How will the builder respond to a client's paid-for inspector's written report?

Builder-Owned or Preferred Mortgage and Title Company:

- Does the builder own the mortgage company that approves loans, or do they utilize third-party lending with which they have a business relationship?

- Does the builder own the title company where the closing between a home buyer and the builder occurs, or does the builder utilize the services of a third-party title with which they have a business relationship?

- Does the builder offer an option incentive for using their preferred or builder-owned mortgage and title company?

After-Closing Service Program:

- Does the builder have a warranty department?

- Does the builder provide the buyer with a Home Owner's Guide?

- Does the builder conduct after-close inspections during the first year? If so, when?

Competitive Pricing:

- What is the price range of my selected builder?

- What standard features are included in the base price?

- Are there any Homeowners' Association Dues?

- What is the property tax rate?

- Is the community located in a MUD or PID District? If so, what is the tax rate?

What Features Agents and Buyers Want in a Community

What follows is a list of features that home buyers and agents want in a new home community:

- Safety.

- Resale value.

- Community amenities.

- Variety of home designs.

- Proximity to services.

- Miscellaneous.

The second half of your task is determining which community to review using the list of abovementioned wants as your guide. Please note that I said community in the singular. I want you to eliminate every community where your selected builder sells new homes but one.

Questions you can ask yourself about the communities in which your selected builder offers homes for sale are as follows:

Safety:

- On a scale of one to ten, how safe is the community?

- If you scored the community less than ten, ask yourself why.

- What have you seen, heard, or read that concerns you about the community?

- Is what you have heard or read coming from a reliable source?

<u>Resale Value</u>:

- How quickly are resale homes in the community selling?

- Are the resale homes increasing in value?

- If so, what is the percentage of the increase?

- If not, why are they not increasing in value?

- How many more homes must the builder sell before the community is sold out?

- Is the builder competing for your future resale home buyers?

- Is the community part of a Public Improvement District (PID) or Municipal Utility District (MUD)? If so, what is the additional annual cost to fund the services?

<u>Community Amenities</u>:

- What, if any, amenities are available?

- Are the amenities easily accessible?

- Are the amenities fully operational?

- What are the HOA fees?

- What is included in the HOA fees?

- What are the HOA restrictions?

<u>Variety of House Designs</u>:

- How many builders are constructing homes within the community?

- What new home designs are available (single-family detached, zero lot line, townhouses, condos, custom and semi-custom homes, etc.)?

- Are there three-car garages?

- Are the garages front, side, or rear-loading?

- Are various exterior designs, including brick, stone, stucco, and siding, available?

- Are there various roof designs available?

- Does the community have a Monotony Code?

<u>Proximity of Services:</u>

- Are services (churches, shopping, schools, daycare, dry cleaners, gas stations, etc.) close to the community?

- If no services are close to the community, how far away are they?

- Are businesses too close to the community, possibly causing congestion issues?

<u>Miscellaneous:</u>

- What type of construction is planned for vacant land that adjoins the community?

- What are the HOA restrictions?

- Is there any public transportation close to the community?

- What is the traffic situation around the community?

- How close are recreational amenities (parks, lakes, ballfields, golf, tennis, and pickleball courts) to the community?

YOUR AGENT PEERS

YOUR NEXT TASK is to discuss and confirm your choice of builder and community with agents who assisted you in developing your list of volume builders. As I write these words, I almost hear you groaning and saying, "*I have decided about the builders and communities I want to refer; why do I need someone to confirm my choice?*"

Seeking confirmation from your peers is not just a formality; it's a sign of respect for their input. You sought help from agents in your office, and many offered their assistance. Sharing your decision and its reasons shows that you valued their help and are committed to integrating new home sales into your business strategy. This confirmation also helps build rapport with your office peers. When you acknowledge the people who helped you get where you are today, you're not just showing gratitude but fostering a culture of mutual support and collaboration.

Chapter Ten Key Takeaways

Chapter Ten provides an overview on how to select the right volume home builder for you and your clients through research. To reinforce your understanding of the material in this chapter, take a few minutes to answer the following three questions? Answering these key takeaways will strengthen your understanding of the chapter's main ideas and aid your ongoing learning about working and partnering with the new home builder community.

1.   What spoke to you most about this chapter?

2.   What insight in these pages made the most significant impression on you?

3.   How will you take what you have learned in this chapter, and put it into action in your pursuit of new home sales?

Finding the Right Community for You and Your Clients

MOVING FORWARD, THE TASKS you will be asked to accomplish are not passive; they are active. You will be asked to experience the community and builder the same way your clients are experiencing it.

As an active participant, you will discover that decisions on the builder and community are based on how each makes you feel. If the builder or community does not access the feeling you seek, you may want to eliminate them. And that is precisely what a homebuyer does. When they are considering a new home, the first thing they do is drive through the community. If the community is different from what they had in mind (does not feel right), they eliminate it as a possibility and move toward another community (new or resale) that has the feel they want.

Selecting a Community

There are three steps required to confirm your community selection, they are:

1. Drive the community.

2. Observe construction quality.

3. Trust your instincts.

DRIVE THE COMMUNITY

You and your clients will choose a community for many reasons, including safety, resale value, community amenities, a diversity of home designs, and proximity to services. As you drive through the community, ask yourself the following questions.

- Does the community feel safe to me? If not, why not?

- Do I feel that the homes being built will retain and increase in value over time?

- Do I feel the community has a cookie-cutter feel?

- How do I think my clients will feel about the community amenities? Or how would my clients feel if there were no community amenities?

- What words would I use to describe the community amenities to my clients?

- Is the community's location close to churches, shopping, daycare, dry cleaners, and a gas station? If not, how will my clients feel about that?

What did each of these questions have in common? Each question was about how clients would feel about the community. I included feel in every question because when a homebuyer buys, they buy the feeling the community conveys. If what they are experiencing does not feel right, they will eliminate the community and move toward something that does. Understanding client emotions is crucial in building a solid connection with your clients.

To prove my point, consider your last community and home tour. When did your client know the community or home you were touring was not what they had in mind?

- Did it happen when you drove into the community?

- Did it happen when you pulled up in front of the house?

- Did it happen when you opened the front door and entered the foyer?

- Did it happen as they toured the home, looking at each room, layout, and condition?

- Did it happen when your client compared the home against other homes they had toured?

How did your client express their dissatisfaction with the house and community? Did they use words like "*The house just doesn't feel right*" or "*The community is not what we had in mind*"? These are not just casual remarks. They are crucial cues to understand what your client is seeing, thinking, and feeling. When you start seeing things from a client's perspective, you're not just doing things for them but empowering them.

Dr. Wayne Dyer wrote in his book *Power of Intentions,* "**When you change the way you look at things, the things you look at change.**" My aim with this book is to ignite a spark in you to transform how you see your clients. This transformation is not just a change; it's a decisive shift in your mindset. A significant step in this conversion is shifting your mindset from that of a seller to that of a buyer. Adopting a buyer's perspective can inspire and serve your clients better.

A Different Mindset

For years, real estate sales focused on what an agent could do to a client. While this selling style satisfied the agents' needs, it fell short of fulfilling clients' needs.

Today's homebuyers are seeking a different type of agent. They want a Realtor willing to do things for them, and this type of selling requires a different mindset. The traditional focus on what an agent could do to a customer is no longer sufficient. It's time to shift to a more client-centered approach. This shift is not just a change in strategy; it's a commitment to serving your clients better and achieving more successful sales.

This book teaches you how to align your sales presentation with your client's home-buying process, reducing or eliminating an adversarial selling and buying relationship. In book three, *Have You Considered the Possibility of a New Home,* the thirteen steps of the home-buying process are revealed and thoroughly explained. Once you understand that your clients have a home-buying process, you will be able to see your interaction with them from a new and more satisfying mindset.

OBSERVE CONSTRUCTION QUALITY

Okay, you have driven the community and asked yourself questions about safety, resale value, community amenities, various home designs, and the community's proximity to services. You are impressed and confident that you could recommend the community to your clients. But wait, what about construction quality?

In Chapter Ten you were asked to review the builders you and your agent peers selected. Your selected criteria included reputation, home-owner satisfaction, mortgage and title options, variety of home designs, quality construction, resale value, communication, features and upgrades, and problem-solving. To narrow your decision, you reviewed your selected builder's website, found and read online reviews, and sought out word-of-mouth reviews. Finally, you answered questions about what you wanted in a builder partner and what a typical home buyer and agent want in a community.

As a real estate agent, you play a pivotal role in finding a community your clients can call home. However, before you finalize your decision about the community, you are responsible for reviewing the quality of homes your selected builder has under construction, the cleanliness of the job sites, and the look of the unfinished and finished homes. Your proactive approach in this process ensures the best for your clients.

Quality

Quality can have both subjective and objective aspects:

- **Subjective**: quality can be subjective, based on personal feelings, tastes, or opinions.

- **Objective**: quality can also be objective, meaning it is based on facts or evidence that can be verified.

So far, you have objectively examined a list of builders you and your agent peers assembled. You selected a community you would feel comfortable referring to. Now it is time to look at the builder you selected subjectively, because that is what your clients do as they drive through the community. For a homebuyer to say "*Yes*" to a builder, the homes under construction must look like they are built with quality in mind.

There are three exterior criteria for forming an opinion on a builder's approach to quality. Those three criteria are:

1. Cleanliness of the job site.

2. Houses under construction.

3. Finished house quality.

CLEANLINESS OF THE JOBSITE

Construction sites are busy hubs of activity where new house progress shapes the community. However, amidst the commotion of a new home development, it is critical that the builder not overlook the importance of a clean work site. An organized and efficient clean construction site ensures a safe working environment for the trades building your client's house, thereby contributing to a quality-built home. A clean construction site is essential to you and your client.

Cleanliness Contributes to Productivity

All new home construction is up against a deadline. One of the best ways for a builder to maintain a construction schedule is cleanliness. Consider for a moment a cluttered, messy, and debris-filled work site. Some trades can navigate other people's messes and complete their assigned tasks, but most cannot.

Most quality-conscious subcontractors want a clean environment in which to work and will follow how others clean up after themselves. If the house is messy when they start, they will add to it when they finish. A good rule that quality-conscious builders follow is that the home must be clean and free of unused construction debris at the end of the workday and ready for tomorrow's subcontractor.

You will know if your builder cares about cleanliness if they have chosen an area for rubbish and waste. A waste disposal bin will be on the driveway or front yard. A best practice for a builder interested in green building is using three bins: one for reuse materials, one for recycling materials, and one for landfill materials.

Remember this as you drive through the community, looking at the cleanliness of a builder's worksite: an organized and clean construction site is a testament to professionalism. It is the foundation of a quality-built home.

HOUSES UNDER CONSTRUCTION

In Book Four of this series, *"The New Home Construction Process,"* I will describe the process in detail and include pictures of what the builder does during each building phase. Until then, you need to know what to look for as you drive through the community and look at your selected builder's homes under construction.

The new home construction process involves sequential tasks. Task B can only be started once Task A is completed. To manage the process, builders use a Gantt Chart or something similar to schedule new home construction. The chart will list all the construction tasks to be performed by various trades, including a start and end date, days scheduled for completion of the task, the progress of the task, and the dates dedicated to the task. The chart includes all the construction phases, including:

- Underground plumbing and electrical

- Foundation

- Framing

- Plumbing, electrical, and HVAC

- Drywall and exterior finishes

- Interior finishes

- Walkthrough inspection and orientation

During your drive through the community, you are tasked with examining three construction phases: foundation, framing, and exterior wall sheathing. What follows is an explanation of each phase.

Foundation

While many types of foundations are possible, the two most popular are concrete slab and pier-and-beam. Of those two, the concrete slab dominates new construction.

Most of today's slab foundations consist of concrete reinforced with rebar or post-tension cables. The builder uses form boards to create the slab's shape. They then put rebar or other steel cables into place. Finally, they pour concrete into the form, allowing openings for plumbing, electrical, and gas lines where necessary.

The advantages of slab foundations include the following:

- **Flexibility**: Since concrete begins as a liquid, the foundation sub-contractor can shape it into almost any shape they need.

- **Durability and strength**: Concrete is among the most robust building materials. Unlike wood, it does not rot and is immune to termites. It is also fire-resistant and remains water-resistant for much longer than most other materials.

However, slab foundations are not without disadvantages, such as the following:

- **Cracking**: Concrete expands and contracts at different temperatures. Over time, this can lead to cracks, damaging the home in other places.

- **Flooding**: Houses built on slab foundations sit close to the ground, making them more susceptible to water infiltration.

One of the most important aspects of any new construction is the grade of the lot. The ground around the foundation should slope away from all sides of the house and promote natural drainage where possible. Areas where water collects near the foundation will eventually cause problems.

YOUR TASK is to locate a house where your selected builder has recently poured a foundation. You can do your inspection from the car. Please notice how the foundation is sitting on the lot. Is the ground around the foundation sloping away from all sides of the house? If the answer is "*Yes,*" the builder has sited the home correctly, and there should be no problems with water infiltration.

Framing

Framing involves the construction of a house's inner support system. Wood, the most common material used for house framing, is easy to find and generally less expensive than other framing materials such as brick, concrete, and steel. Local building codes enforce specifications by the International Residential Code (IRC), which indicates requirements and measurements for single and multi-family house framing projects to ensure structurally sound construction.

Stick framing is a traditional method of building a new home. The structure is assembled on-site using lumber cut to various sizes. What follows are some characteristics of stick framing:

- The construction begins after the foundation and sill plate are in place. The foundation supports the first-floor platform, first-floor walls, and the second-floor if the home is two stories high. The lumber used for stick framing is typically 2x4 or 2x6, placed 16 or 24 inches apart.

- Stick-built homes can be custom-designed, allowing the buyer to personalize the layout and amenities. Personalization might include some of the following:

- Cathedral ceilings

- Ceilings greater than nine feet tall

- Larger overhangs

- Taller roof pitches

- Hip roof designs

- Radiant floor heating

- Customized tile designs

- Metal roofs

- Extensive exterior stone, brick, or cement board siding

- Complex floor designs

Stick framing is a traditional method and a wise financial choice. It's a cost-effective option that can be built on any plot of land, making it a savvy investment for your client's new home. While some may question the insulation quality, weather resistance, and maintenance of wooden-framed houses, the correct construction methods and materials can effectively address these concerns.

YOUR TASK is to locate a house where your selected builder has just begun framing. You can conduct your inspection from the car. Notice how the house is framed.

- Is the framing complete or under construction?

- If the framing is unfinished, where are the remaining building materials stored?

- Are they exposed to the weather in the garage or outside?

- If the framing is complete, are the roofers installing the roof?

Your answers to these questions provide insight into whether the builder you have chosen is considering how the weather might affect building materials, which may alter the quality of the home being built.

Exterior Wall Sheathing

Exterior wall sheathing provides structural support and is crucial in insulating and protecting the home from the elements. Five options are available.

Plywood Sheathing

It is often used for its affordability and versatility. It comprises thin, glued veneer wood to form a durable panel. Plywood sheathing offers excellent structural integrity and can withstand high winds and impact. A disadvantage is that, over time, the layers within plywood may return to their natural state of being round. This can cause the edges to curl, compromising the integrity of the material and adversely affecting its performance.

Oriented Strand Board (OSB)

OSB is another commonly used exterior wall sheathing material. It is made from tiny strands of wood oriented in different directions, compressed, and bonded with resins. OSB offers similar structural properties to plywood sheathing but at a lower cost. A disadvantage of OSB over plywood sheathing is moisture damage.

Fiber Cement Sheathing

It is a composite material made from cement, sand, and cellulose fibers. It offers excellent durability and resistance to fire, insects, and rot. A disadvantage to fiber cement sheathing is that it is more expensive than other options.

Gypsum Board Sheathing

This lightweight and cost-effective option for exterior wall sheathing is made from gypsum board reinforced with fiberglass mats. It provides good insulation properties and contributes to the house's energy efficiency. A disadvantage is that it is less durable than the other options.

Foam-Insulating Sheathing

It is a good option for homeowners looking to improve their energy efficiency. It is made from rigid foam panels that provide excellent insulation and reduce thermal bridging. A disadvantage is that it does not provide structural support and needs to be combined with other sheathing materials.

YOUR TASK is to locate a house where your selected builder has installed exterior wall sheathing over the house frame. From your car, determine what exterior sheathing the builder has chosen. The type of exterior sheathing a builder chooses depends on budget, climate, design preferences, and structural requirements. If the builder builds for the first-time buyer market, plywood or oriented strand board is the most cost-effective option. If the builder offers energy-efficient homes, foam-insulating sheathing is the right choice. If the builder wants to provide clients with better durability, fiber cement or plywood sheathing is the best choice.

As you can tell, each type of exterior sheathing has pros and cons. When you look at the sheathing, consider your typical client.

- Are they on a tight budget?

- Are they looking for energy efficiency?

- Do they want a home built with durability and strength in mind?

Your client is the only one who can answer these questions. In Book Three, *"Have You Considered the Possibility of New?"* I will provide a discovery process to uncover your client's needs and wants.

The builder you choose for your client may or may not build with the product that will satisfy their needs. But it would be best if you remembered that the lack of a single product does not mean the builder you choose is not suitable for them. A home comprises hundreds of products; wall sheathing is just one of those products.

Your next task is to discover if the builder uses a house wrap and, if so, what brand they use.

House Wrap

House wrap is a weatherization membrane that creates an air and moisture barrier.

Uncontrolled air infiltration lowers the wall assembly's effective R-value, which can affect the home's energy efficiency. House wrap also establishes a protective envelope against moisture infiltration into the wall cavities. A moisture build-up within a home's wall cavities can lead to wood rot and costly repairs. High humidity can also cause mold to grow, which is unhealthy for the home's occupants. To minimize air infiltration and prevent moisture accumulation within the wall assembly, every home's design should include a house wrap.

YOUR TASK is to locate a house where your selected builder has installed a house wrap over the exterior wall sheathing. From your car, determine what house wrap the builder has chosen. Make a note of the brand, and then, on your computer, research the builder's choice. There are many different brands of house wrap, and each has its benefits.

Builder Products

You might consider adding a bookmark folder to your preferred search engine and title it, Builder Products. This is an excellent way to locate products that your selected builder uses quickly. With this information, you can demonstrate your knowledge of construction and the features and benefits of home-building products when your clients ask about the products the builder is using.

The last task on your builder quality review is finding finished homes constructed by your selected builder.

FINISHED HOUSE QUALITY

Okay, you have driven the community and looked at homes under construction. You feel confident that the builder you have chosen is someone you can refer. However, one more review is necessary, and that is a drive-by assessment of your selected builders' finished homes.

This last examination may be the most important because it is what your client does before visiting the model home. Suppose the community and the builder's homes differ from what they are looking for. In that case, they will leave the neighborhood and find a place that meets their decision-making criteria for a home, homesite, community, and location.

A list of things to review as you drive the community, assessing finished homes.

- House designs

- Quality of finished houses

- Landscape package

- Condition of inventory houses

- Quality of competitors' houses

What follows is a brief explanation of what you should be looking for.

House Designs

Most volume builders offer five to seven new home designs. The interior of each home design has the same room layout, which can be altered by purchasing options and structural upgrades. The exterior may have three to four different elevation combinations. The difference will be a combination of brick, stone, stucco, and siding. The exterior elevation will also include a combination of varying roof pitches.

YOUR TASK is to examine the home designs to determine whether the builder is repeating the same house or has built a community with various elevation designs.

To complete this task, I want you to consider whether the builder adheres to a monotony code. Earlier in this book, I wrote that this code mandates sufficient differences in house designs, color schemes, and exterior finishes, including brick, stone, siding, and roof design. Most new home volume builders abide by the following:

- Homes of the same elevation may be built, provided at least one home of a different elevation is built in between. If across the street, the same elevation must be one home over.

- The same exterior siding and masonry color may be installed, provided two homes of different color selections are built between them. If across the street, the same color must be two homes over.

- In cul-de-sac circles, all homes must be significantly different.

As you observe your selected builder's finished homes, ask yourself, ***"Is the builder adhering to a monotony code?"*** If they are, great; if not, then be aware that this community and builder may not suit you and your client.

Quality of Finished Houses

This examination is a little tricky because when assessing the quality of a finished house, especially from your car and not up close, you must remember that your assessment is subjective (based on personal feelings).

With that in mind, what follows are some things you can observe that will help you form a judgment about the quality of the finished homes:

- Drainage.

- Gutters.

- Exterior trim.

- Concrete finish.

- Roofing shingles.

- Painting and caulking.

- Window finish (aluminum, vinyl, wood, and color finishes).

- Landscaping.

- Sod.

- Fencing.

- Front door system.

YOUR TASK is to review finished houses in an established part of the community, not in a construction zone.

Home Buyers Look To Eliminate

Within a community, you will find houses under construction, occupied homes, and houses built for the market. Your focus is on occupied homes. As you look at those homes, remember that your clients see what you see.

As I stated, a potential new home buyer drives through the neighborhood looking at occupied homes before visiting with the on-site salesperson. Suppose the houses do not look like what they had in mind. In that case, they eliminate the community and move toward another development (new or resale) that includes the type of house they seek.

Looking at finished houses is a decisive moment for a home buyer. So, as you drive through the community, pretend you are a home buyer and ask yourself the following questions:

- Do the homes have a quality feel to them?

- Are the homes correctly sited on the lot?

- Do the homes have gutters?

- Do you see any cracks in the driveway, walkway, etc.? What exterior elevations are you seeing?

- What about roof pitches? Are they varied, or are they all the same?

- Are there other builders building in the area? If other builders are in the community, are their homes distinguishable from your selected builder's homes?

- Can you tell the difference between your chosen builder and the competition? If so, what is the difference? Does the difference add value to the home?

The answers to these questions determine whether or not you can recommend the builder and community to your clients. You are looking at what your client is purchasing. It is not the model with one hundred thousand dollars of options and upgrades. It is a house purchased by a client similar to your client.

Congratulations if what you see captures the feeling your clients are looking for; you may have found a community and a builder with whom you can partner.

TRUST YOUR INSTINCTS

Pause for a few moments and go back and reread the last sentence. What word or words stand out? For me, the two keywords are "*May have*." Your decision is not final until you can, without reservation, answer the question in the affirmative that the community and builder are suitable for you and your future new home build clients.

To answer that question, you must trust your instincts. Trusting your instincts, or gut feelings, means making decisions based on your inner voice and intuition rather than external data. Gut feelings are a valuable tool for making good choices and can be mentally, physically, and emotionally beneficial.

Throughout this book, I have stated that home buyers buy a feeling they get from the home, homesite, community, location, a financing program, or the builder if they are considering a new home. If what they see is incongruent with their gut feeling, they will eliminate what they are looking at and move on. It is crucial to understand that clients are not looking to buy when they tour a community or home. They are looking to eliminate.

As you decide whether this is the right builder and community for you and your clients, please do what your clients do: look at the builder and community through the lens of elimination. If what you see gives you a positive feeling, trust it and make the referral. If you feel negative, trust your instincts and move on to the next opportunity. Remember that builders and communities are like buses; miss one, wait a few minutes, and another builder and community will show up.

CHAPTER ELEVEN KEY TAKEAWAYS

Chapter Eleven provides an overview of the key aspects you need to know about to find the right community for you and your clients. To reinforce your understanding of the material in this chapter, take a few minutes to answer the following three questions? Answering these key takeaways will strengthen your understanding of the chapter's main ideas and aid your ongoing learning about working and partnering with the new home builder community.

1.   What spoke to you most about this chapter?

2.   What insight in these pages made the most significant impression on you?

3.   How will you take what you have learned in this chapter, and put it into action in your pursuit of new home sales?

Choosing the Right Volume Builder for You and Your Clients

S O FAR, I HAVE had you focus on homes under construction, and your examination was done from the car. Now, **YOUR TASK** is to walk through several houses under construction and at least one finished house built for the market. The houses under construction should be pre-dry-wall, and the inventory home must be complete and ready to move into. This direct observation of what the builder is capable of forms a basis of knowledge that you can communicate to your clients. I refer to this activity as experiencing the experience. There is no substitute for understanding what a builder does than experiencing what they build and how they make it first-hand.

HOUSE UNDER CONSTRUCTION

To successfully inspect a house under construction, direct your attention to the following:

- Safety

- Planning

Safety

A construction site can be dangerous, so consider your safety before entering a house under construction. This means always wearing the appropriate personal protective equipment (PPE). Some examples of PPE that you might consider purchasing include:

- **<u>Hard hat</u>** – Protects the head from falling objects. Hard hats should comply with the ANSI Z89.1 standard.

- **<u>Safety glasses</u>**—These protect the eyes from flying debris. They should comply with the ANSI Z87 standard and have side shields. Prescription glasses are not considered safe unless they meet the ANSI Z87 standard.

- **<u>Safety footwear</u>** – Protects the feet from heavy objects and punctures. Safety boots should have steel toecaps.

Additionally, think about purchasing a coverall to wear over your work clothes. A construction site can be very muddy, as new houses at the pre-drywall stage won't always have driveways or sidewalks.

Planning

Please understand that walking into a house under construction without permission might be against the builder's Policies and Procedures. So, before entering the home, please stop at the construction trailer and seek permission from the construction supervisor or, better yet, ask them to accompany you. When approaching the community builder, remember their primary responsibility is to adhere to a construction schedule and complete homes according to established deadlines. With that thought in mind, consider the following introduction and request.

***

Hi, my name is (your name). I am a real estate agent for (broker name). Here is my business card. I want to build my real estate business through new home sales, and I need your help. With your permission, I want to walk through a house under construction in the pre-drywall phase. I can do it myself, or if you have time in your schedule, you could accompany me and answer any questions I might have. You could also point out features in the house that contrast with how your competition builds. Can you assist me today?

***

What follows is what this introduction and request accomplished:

- You introduced yourself and the broker you are affiliated with, and your business card demonstrates that you are a licensed real estate agent.

- You stated what you want and that you need help to achieve what you want.

- You identified the phase of construction you want to examine.

- You asked for permission, but could do it yourself if necessary.

- You asked, if schedule permitted, for the builder to accompany you to answer questions and point out features that are better than the competition.

- You asked for assistance today.

In this book's Introduction, I wrote, "***Agents willing to do what their peers are unwilling to do are unique in the real estate industry***." The introduction and request I described above is when you are asked to do something difficult. Something that many agents who read this book will be unwilling to do. Unfortunately, that is a missed opportunity to meet the construction supervisor who will manage the construction of your clients' new homes. This introduction sets you apart from all the other Realtors with whom the on-site agent comes in contact. Additionally, this introduction demonstrates the respect you have for the construction supervisor, their time, and the knowledge they possess.

I commit to you that if you do what I am asking you to do, it will pay dividends for years to come, especially when you need the help of the construction supervisor to solve a construction issue.

After you ask for assistance today, please pause and wait for a reply. There are only two possible responses to your question: "*Yes, I have time today, or No, I don't have time today.*" Both answers are acceptable. Let's look at each response and how you can use it.

Community Supervisor Responses

Supervisor response: *"Yes, I have time today."*

Your response: *That is what I wanted to hear. Before we start, let me share with you my purpose. I aim to build my real estate business through new home sales. To accomplish my goal, I am visiting several communities to experience the quality of the homes under construction and the quality of their finished inventory homes. If what I see and hear is favorable, I want to take the next step and visit with the on-site salesperson to learn more about why I should recommend the community and builder to my clients. Do you have any questions for me? If not, let's get started.*

Before proceeding let's examine the reply to the construction supervisor.

- The reply defines your purpose by setting an expectation.

- The reply alerts the construction manager that you are visiting several communities, letting the supervisor know you are serious about selling new homes and that other builders are being considered.

- The reply informs the community construction manager that you have not spoken to the on-site salesperson yet. What you see and hear as you tour a home under construction and a finished inventory home will determine whether that meeting will occur.

- The reply allows the superintendent to ask questions.

- The reply establishes a call to action.

Once again, I want to take a pause for an explanation before moving on to Builder Response #2. I want to clarify what I mean by setting expectations. Setting clear expectations about your goal is paramount to your success. If I were to boil down the idea of setting and managing clear expectations into one word, that would be alignment. When you and the construction manager align on your goals, you can move forward together confidently. If you fail to set an expectation, you turn control of the review over to the supervisor, thereby misaligning yourself with them.

Stop reading and ask yourself, "***Who do I want controlling the construction walkthrough, me or the builder?***" I hope your answer is you because, as you will soon find out, you have things you want to know about the builder's construction practices that will help you make an informed decision. If you leave it up to the construction supervisor, you may hear things you are not interested in. You either take control or be controlled. Like all things in life, the choice is yours. I hope you choose wisely.

Let's examine how you might respond when the construction manager responds negatively, because you have two options. Both options will work depending on your schedule. Remember, you are in control. You get to choose how you want to proceed.

***

Supervisor response: *"No, I don't have time today."*

Your response: *I understand and appreciate you taking a few moments to talk with me today. I know a thousand things are competing for your time. If today doesn't work, is there another day this week we can schedule a construction walkthrough? What day and time is open on your schedule? I will come early in the morning or late in the day. This is important to me, and I am willing to do whatever it takes to succeed in selling new homes.*

Like the other proposed responses, let's examine why this reply sets you apart from other agents with whom the construction supervisor interacts.

- The reply accepts what you heard and thanks the supervisor for listening to your request.

- The reply acknowledges that the supervisor is busy.

- The reply asks for an alternative date to work with the supervisor's schedule.

- The reply alerts the supervisor that you are willing to meet early or late, separating you from other real estate agents.

- The reply stated that you want to build your real estate business through new home sales.

As I stated earlier, you are in control. If you feel confident enough to walk the house under construction without the benefit of a community construction manager, use the following response.

***

Supervisor response: *"No, I don't have time today."*

Your response: *I understand and appreciate you taking a few moments to talk with me today. I know a thousand things are competing for your time. If today doesn't work, will you permit me to inspect a home in the pre-drywall construction phase on my own? I have protective equipment because I know a construction site can be dangerous. Do I have your permission?*

This response is different from the other two responses because you are asking for permission, which sets you apart, in the eyes of the construction supervisor, from the other agents they meet. Let's examine why this response works so well and puts you in a position to achieve your goals.

- Reply offers both appreciation and understanding.

- Reply acknowledges how busy a community construction manager is.

- Reply seeks permission to inspect the home on your own.

- Reply conveys that you have the construction knowledge to review a house in the pre-drywall phase.

- Reply informs the construction supervisor that you have the proper protective equipment to keep you safe.

Setting Community Supervisor Expectations

Before explaining what to look for as you walk through a house in the pre-drywall phase, I want to set an expectation for how you should use the responses I wrote. I do not expect you to memorize those responses. I wrote the responses so you would have an example of communicating professionally with the construction manager. Each response included the following:

- Respect for the person.

- Respect for their time.

- Respect for the position they hold.

- A goal to make new home sales a part of your real estate business.

- An understanding of new home construction.

- An understanding that a construction site can be dangerous.

- An understanding that a construction manager is a busy person handling a multitude of trades, suppliers, and home buyers.

Before meeting the construction supervisor for the first time, consider what you want to say and how you want to say it. Your choice of words is entirely up to you. Be respectful, communicate an appreciation for the supervisor's time, and establish a positive working relationship. And, most importantly, communicate your desire to make new home sales an essential part of your real estate business.

PRE-DRYWALL WALKTHROUGH

As you prepare for the pre-drywall walkthrough, you have two options. The first scenario involves a walkthrough with the assistance of the construction supervisor, and the second scenario has you performing the walkthrough examination on your own. What follows includes best practices for each situation.

Assisted Pre-Drywall Walkthrough

There are three steps to a successful assisted pre-drywall walkthrough. They are:

1. Set walkthrough expectations.

2. Take photographs and notes.

3. Record photographs and notes in a Digital Builder Binder.

Each step communicates your seriousness to the construction supervisor. The first step, setting walkthrough expectations, reveals your purpose; the second step, taking pictures and notes, shows you are listening with your ears and eyes; and the third step, recording photographs and notes in a Digital Builder Binder, provides a place for you to recall what you learned during the pre-drywall walkthrough.

Here is a brief explanation of each step.

Establish Pre-Drywall Walkthrough Expectations

To set an expectation, you must identify your purpose. Here are some things you might consider including in your expectations.

- Pre-drywall inspection review that includes:

  - Framing

  - HVAC

  - Electrical

  - Plumbing

  - Insulation

- Identify any construction and option changes permitted by the builder at this phase of construction.

- The builder's willingness to allow third-party inspections.

- Permission to take photographs and notes.

Here is an example of setting a pre-drywall walkthrough expectation with the construction supervisor before entering the house.

***

Before we start, I want to share my purpose with you. Today, I aim to learn about the following construction systems and their related benefits: framing, HVAC, electrical, plumbing, and how the house is insulated. Additionally, is it okay to take photographs and notes to help me remember what I've seen and heard? Do you have any questions for me?

***

Once again, and it is worth repeating, I do not expect you to memorize what I've written, nor do I want you to. I want you to understand the purpose of the walkthrough. The pre-drywall walkthrough gathers information so you can make an informed decision about the builder. The type of information needed is included in the expectations communicated to the construction supervisor.

You can convey what you want in any way that feels comfortable. Just be sure to include everything you need to make an informed decision. To remind you, consider adding a note-taking app to your phone. Create a folder within the app and title it Pre-Dry Walkthrough. Then, add a page and title it Pre-Drywall Walkthrough Expectations. Use the page to take notes during the walkthrough.

- Pre-drywall inspection review

  - Framing

  - HVAC

  - Electrical

  - Plumbing

- ○ Insulation

- Construction and option changes

- Third-party inspections

- Photographs and notes

- Construction differences from the competition

If you do not hear what you want, respectfully redirect the conversation to your stated expectations. Don't be intimidated; you are in control. Your goal is to build your real estate business through new home sales, and choosing the right builder for you and your client is paramount to building a successful new home sales business.

Take Photographs and Notes

When you tour a home in the pre-drywall phase, there is much to observe, so snap plenty of pictures and capture what you hear in your notes. Pay particular attention to the placement of HVAC, electrical, and plumbing. Most of what you are looking at is built to code, but some builders will add features that are only recognizable if identified. Be sure to ask about construction differences from their competitors. If the construction supervisor identifies a difference, take notes and repeat what you heard for confirmation.

In Book Six, *Negotiating with a New Home Builder*, you will learn the importance of comparing and contrasting one builder against another. Information acquired during your community and builder reviews is necessary to do this effectively. When a construction supervisor identifies a difference, ask what the difference will mean to your clients. In other words, what is the benefit? If you have questions, ask for clarification. Be sure to repeat what you heard for verification.

Third-Party Inspection

Constructing a new home will be one of the most significant investments your client will ever make. As their agent, ensuring the quality and integrity of the construction process is crucial for your client's peace of mind and your own. One of the best ways to achieve this is through qualified independent third-party inspections at critical construction phases. These inspections offer an impartial assessment of the builder's work and ensure compliance with building codes, helping to avoid costly repairs or disputes in the future.

While some builders allow independent inspections, others may include clauses limiting or outright disallowing them in the construction contract. This can leave your client wondering what the builder is hiding. So, you must determine whether third-party inspectors are welcome and how the builder will respond to the inspector's report.

Don't be shy about enquiring about the use of third-party Inspectors. Most reputable builders will accept the presence of a third-party inspection with some restrictions.

Scheduling

Builders maintain a construction schedule, so the inspector must complete their inspection per the builder's schedule. For a pre-drywall inspection, there is a tight window between the completion of framing, HVAC, electrical, plumbing, and insulation installation. Ask the construction supervisor how long the inspector will have to complete the inspection and file a report that can be acted upon (in most construction situations, this may only be one or two days). Additionally, find out who is responsible for alerting the inspector that the home is ready for inspection. In most cases, it will be the responsibility of the homeowner. So, before your client decides to purchase the services of a third-party inspector, they need to accept the task of communicating with the inspector promptly.

Third-Party Inspection Report

A quality builder appreciates learning about construction issues before installing drywall. However, not all defects in the report may be acceptable to the builder. The best scenario for your client is that they present the written report and then accompany the builder as they inspect the defects identified, allowing them to agree or disagree on whether the defect will be fixed.

Review of Corrected Defects

Ask the builder if your client can review any defects approved for repair or replacement before installing drywall. Once again, your client must work within the builder's schedule.

I recommend that you and your client consider hiring a Third-Party Inspector for the drywall and closing phase. For pricing, Google *Third-Party New Home Inspectors*. I suggest you contact several and ask for references and a sample report. But before you and your client decide, confirm with your client that they take responsibility for scheduling the inspector.

Final Thoughts

When you finish the walkthrough, take a few minutes to review your notes. Ask the construction supervisor if you missed anything important. If not, ask them to open an inventory home for you to inspect and invite them to tour the house with you to answer any questions. If they decline because of time constraints, no worries. Thank them for their time, and tell them you look forward to working with them soon.

Now, congratulate yourself. Through words and deeds, you have demonstrated that you are different. You are not an agent who shows up only at the contract signing and is never seen again until closing. You are a professional agent and someone to be respected.

Unassisted Pre-Drywall Walkthrough

If you have never sold or have limited experience with new home sales, I recommend not doing an unassisted pre-drywall walkthrough. The purpose of the walkthrough is not just to see what is behind the drywall; it is to understand how the builder is constructing the home so you can confidently refer the builder to your clients.

I want you to see the pre-drywall walkthrough as a learning experience, not just something to cross off your to-do list. Waiting a day or two or even a week for the construction supervisor is fine. Remember, you are building a new home sales business, and the construction knowledge you acquire will be worth the wait.

Here are three ways to get construction knowledge about the pre-drywall walkthrough, other than the construction supervisor:

Third-Party Inspector

I have written several times that I am in favor of hiring a third-party inspector for at least two inspections:

- Pre-Drywall Inspection

- Pre-Closing Inspection

Therefore, I recommend contacting a third-party inspector and telling them you want to build your real estate business through new home sales and need their help. Explain that you have little or no new home construction experience. Ask if you could shadow them on a pre-drywall inspection. Most new home inspectors will welcome this opportunity to educate you and earn future referrals. What follows is an example of the things you will learn about during a third-party pre-drywall inspection:

- Framing of the entire structure, interior, exterior, and roof.

- Electrical system, including wiring and junction boxes

- Plumbing system, including supply, drain lines, and shower drain pan.

- Mechanical HVAC system, including HVAC ducts, dryer, and exhaust vents.

During the inspection, take plenty of pictures and notes. If you don't understand something, ask questions until you do. Remember that you aim to acquire construction knowledge to refer a builder confidently.

YouTube Pre-Drywall Inspection Videos

Many YouTube videos walk you through the pre-drywall inspection process step-by-step. They feature a third-party inspector or builder. These videos are five to ten minutes in length and contain helpful information. To find these videos, go to YouTube.com and enter *Pre-Drywall Inspection*. Here are a couple of titles that I found:

- What to Look for in a Pre-Drywall Walkthrough – 9 minutes

- What to Look for in a Pre-Drywall Walk-Thru – 8 minutes

- New Build- Phase 2, Pre-Sheetrock Inspection – 10 minutes

Watching these videos is a good first step. They teach you what to look for. While watching the video, take plenty of notes about each construction phase. However, there is no substitute for an actual walkthrough. So, after watching several videos, reach out to the construction supervisor or third-party inspector and schedule a time to shadow them on a pre-drywall inspection.

Membership and Mentoring

This third option is the most time-consuming and has a financial cost, but it will yield the best results. It begins with a phone call to your local Home Builder Association. Once connected, ask for the membership director. The call is for informational purposes, so be prepared to do the following:

- Introduce yourself and your purpose.

- Enquire about the cost of becoming a member.

- Find out about membership benefits.

- Ask about new home construction education programs.

- Question whether the association has a mentorship program.

- Request a new membership information packet.

Here is an example of what you might say:

***

Hi, my name is (your name). I am a real estate agent for (broker name). I want to build my real estate business through new home sales, and I need the help of the Home Builders' Association to achieve my goal. Do you have time to answer some questions now, or would it be best to schedule an in-person meeting? If you feel an in-person meeting makes the most sense, please send me a new membership packet. I promise to read it, and I will be prepared for our meeting.

***

I believe an in-person meeting would be best for you and the Membership Director because real estate agents rarely, if ever, seek help directly from the Builders' Association. While the Membership Director will be accommodating, they will also be shocked by your phone call.

Phone or In-Person Meeting Preparation

This initial phone call sets you apart from most Realtors they have met. So, you must prepare for this in-person or phone meeting because it may be the catalyst that ignites your new home sales business.

What follows are my recommendations for your first meeting:

1. **Communicate the purpose of the meeting**:

   a. Build your real estate business through new home sales.

2. **Questions to ask:**

   a. **Membership**

      i. What is the cost for a real estate agent to become an association member?

      ii. How can I reduce the cost of membership?

      iii. Are there any other real estate agent members?

      iv. If so, are those agents affiliated with a broker who is a member?

      v. As a member of the Association, can I be on a committee?

   b. **Education**

      i. What new home construction education classes are available through the association?

      ii. I am only interested in construction classes. I reviewed the website and see that you offer them. Can I attend the classes that benefit me, or must I attend all the construction classes?

      iii. Does the association conduct any classes on a construction site?

    iv. What is the cost of attending a class?

c. **Networking**

    i. What networking events does the Association sponsor?

    ii. As an Association member, can I obtain a contact list of other members, including builders and associate members?

    iii. Are there any restrictions on contacting members via email or text?

d. **Mentoring**

    i. I aim to build my real estate business through new sales. Can you refer me to several builder members who might be willing to mentor me?

    ii. If not, could I include my request in your weekly newsletter or purchase ad space?

e. **Miscellaneous**

    i. Can I serve on committees? If so, who do I contact to let them know I am interested in serving?

    ii. Where can I find a list of committees and councils and their mission?

I can imagine your reaction to my recommendations. I have written several times about being different. Well, joining and becoming an active member of your local Home Builders' Association is different. It is not for every Realtor, but you are not just the run-of-the-mill agent. You want to build your real estate business through new home sales. To do that, you must become known in the community of new home builders. There is no better way to do that than networking with builders and their suppliers. Through membership, you can secure new home builder listings and acquire resale listings and referrals from suppliers. I have a favorite saying, ***"If you want to catch fish, go where the fish are."*** There is no better fishing hole than your local Home Builders' Association.

I have given you three options:

1. Shadowing a third-party new home inspector.

2. Watching pre-drywall walkthrough videos on YouTube.

3. Becoming an active member of your local Home Builders' Association and finding a builder willing to mentor you.

My advice is to do all three. Your knowledge of new home construction will set you apart from other real estate agents. Will my suggestions take time? Yes, they will take time, but the price of success is time. So, before you commit to building a new home sales business, ask yourself, *"How serious am I about building my real estate business through new home sales?"* If your answer is *"I am serious,"* then find the time to partake in all three options.

Digital Builder Binder

The final step to a successful assisted or unassisted pre-drywall walkthrough is recording your photographs and notes in a Digital Builder Binder. Throughout this chapter, I have shared many ideas that will separate you from other agents. The Digital Builder Binder is one of those ideas that will elevate you as an expert in new home sales. You will become the go-to person in your office for new home information. The Digital Builder Binder is simple to implement but requires constant updating because builder information changes as fast as the market changes. What follows is an explanation of how to assemble a Digital Builder Binder.

Open your computer and do the following:

- Create a folder and title it My Builders.

- Open the My Builders folder and create a new folder; title it (name of builder you are partnering with, for example, Lennar Homes).

- Please create a separate folder for every builder you partner with. You will have five My Builder Folders if you have five builder partners.

  - Open a My Builder Folder and create the following separate Subfolders:

    - **Builder Notes**

    - **House Photographs**

      - Home Under Construction

      - House Plan #1

      - House Plan #2

      - House Plan #3

- ○ Etc.

- **Finished Houses**

  - ○ House Plan #1

  - ○ House Plan #2

  - ○ House Plan #3

  - ○ Etc.

- **Builder Brochures**

- **Builder Standard Features Sheet**

- **Builder Lot Listings**

- **Builder Price Sheets**

- **Builder Emails**

- **Builder Options and Pricing**

- **Builder Contract and Addenda**

- **Builder Warranty**

- **Builder Promotions**

- **Builder Inventory Houses**

  - ○ House Plan #1

  - ○ House Plan #2

- House Plan #3

- Etc.

You will create the same subfolders under each builder partner's folder. You may also need to add subfolders to a subfolder. An example is Builder Photographs, because you may take pictures of homes under construction and finished homes.

Congratulations! You have created a Digital Builder Binder and now have a place to store the builder information you acquire while interacting with the on-site salesperson. This gathered information will be beneficial when comparing and contrasting the differences between builders. Everything you need will be at your fingertips.

As I stated, the idea is easy to implement but requires timely updating. When you complete a pre-drywall inspection, an inventory home walk-through, a model home visit with the on-site agent, and receive email updates from the builder on pricing, new products, promotions, etc., they must be scanned and filed. Like all successful businesses, there are administrative tasks that must be completed. The Digital Builder Binder is one of those responsibilities. I believe embracing this idea will increase your sales, income, and credibility.

INVENTORY HOME WALKTHROUGH

New home builders understand that most clients they represent need a home now and cannot wait for a home to be built. For this reason, volume builders construct a percentage of their annual sales on speculation. The percentage varies by builder, and it is something you will want to discuss with the builder's on-site salesperson. I recommend you partner with volume builders who maintain three to five speculative homes per community in various stages of development. A builder's inventory level signals how vital real estate agents are to their business.

A good rule of thumb for builders is that when an inventory home is sold, another one is immediately started. This strategy is good for you and your clients and is also a good indicator that the volume builder is financially sound.

Builders who construct inventory homes as part of their sales strategy have procedures they follow to ensure the homes they build on speculation sell quickly. They include:

- Lot selection

- House design

- Options

- Pricing

- Marketing

- Negotiation

What follows is a brief look at each one of those procedures.

Lot Selection

Most builders select filler lots to construct their inventory houses. A filler lot sits between two under-construction or finished homes. They will also choose lots that back up to roadways, commercial areas, high-tension lines, and maybe even railroad lines. Builders understand these are undesirable lots; therefore, they will market these homes differently from speculative homes built on better-located lots.

Marketing may include lower pricing, additional options, structural changes, upgraded landscaping, closing costs, etc. If you have a client looking for a great deal, look no further than lots with some visual or sound challenges. The benefit to your client is instant equity.

House Design

When a builder decides to include inventory homes in their sales strategy, they need those houses to sell quickly, preferably before the house is complete. The reason is financial. The longer the home stays unsold, the higher the interest carried and maintenance cost for the builder. Therefore, their design choice starts with choosing an exterior elevation that will appeal to most of the market.

I have written about how a home buyer selects a community and builder, but it is worth repeating. When prospective buyers consider a new home, they will find a location that fits their lifestyle. Once they have narrowed down the area, they will drive through the community and look at the homes being built there. If the curb appeal, meaning the general appearance of the exterior, comes close to what they have in mind, they will want to look inside the home to ensure the inside appearance matches what they see on the outside. Builders understand this behavior and will select a house design that entices people to visit the model home to learn more.

Walkthrough with Construction Supervisor

Unlike a prospective buyer, you must walk through an inventory home to learn more before you meet with the builder's on-site salesperson. This walkthrough aims to decide whether a visit to the model home is warranted. Therefore, ask the community construction manager to open a speculative home. The supervisor doesn't need to accompany you, but if they have time, invite them to do so. Before touring the inside, set the following expectations with them.

***

Before we go inside, please point out one thing on the exterior that sets you apart from what the competition offers. Then, when we get inside, please identify any options or structural changes that have been added and are not included in the house's base price. Finally, can my clients make any construction changes or add options to a completed inventory home? If so, what construction changes can be made, and what optional choices can be added? One last thing: is it okay if I take photos and notes? Do you have any questions? If not, let's get started.

***

This expectation asks several essential questions. You must understand these to communicate builder inventory home procedures to your clients. Nothing disappoints a client more than finding a home they like, only to find out that adding an option or making a construction change (for example, changing countertops or cabinet style) is impossible once the house is complete.

The phrase **"Knowledge is Power"** is accurate when communicating a new home builder's procedure to a client. Remember, not all home builders follow the same guidelines, so learning what you can and cannot do with a finished home will set you apart in the eyes of the builder and your client.

What this expectation uncovers:

- A construction feature on the exterior that differs from what a competitive builder in the community offers. This knowledge is essential when you compare and contrast builders in the same community.

- Options and structural changes the builder has added to the base price. Builders typically add about ten to twelve percent of the base price in options or structural changes. In other words, if the base price is four hundred thousand dollars, the builder will add forty thousand dollars in options and structural changes. The three most popular options are upgrading floors, countertops, and cabinets.

- Learning whether any options or constructional changes can be made to the house. This is essential information because your client will want to change or add an option to what the builder has chosen. A change might be as simple as adding blinds to the windows or as complicated as changing kitchen cabinets and countertops. A builder's decision about changes depends on the age of the inventory home. If the house was completed within the last sixty days, the builder will most likely say no to any changes, but if the house has been on the market for many months, the builder may be open to making some constructional changes.

Please note that the construction supervisor will always say no to changes because they mean more work for them. Remember that you are asking about changes for informational purposes, so whatever the construction supervisor says is not the final word. The builder makes the decision, not the supervisor or the on-site salesperson.

Walkthrough Without Construction Supervisor

If the construction supervisor cannot accompany you, there are three things you need to know before touring the home on your own. They are:

- The options and structural changes were added to the home.

- The builder's policy on a completed home as it relates to changes or additions.

- The construction differences between competing builders in the same community.

Here is an example of how you might ask about all three:

***

I understand you are busy, and I appreciate the time you have given me. There are just a couple of things I need to know. What options or changes have been added to the house? Because it is a completed home, can my clients add options or make minor changes to the house? An example might be adding blinds, changing countertops, or possibly flooring. And finally, from a construction perspective, can you tell me the significant differences between your houses and those built by the competition?

***

Be patient and give the supervisor time to answer your questions. If necessary, ask them to pull the inventory home file. Don't feel like you are asking too much; the information you want is needed to describe the home clearly to a client. Too many agents walk through inventory homes without knowing what options and structural changes have been made to the house. Additionally, they don't know the builder's policy concerning adding options once a home is complete.

I promise you that your clients will want to know what has been added and if any changes are possible. The best time to inform a client about a builder's policy is when the question is asked. The worst thing you can do is delay the answer by telling your client you are unsure and saying. *"Let's ask the salesperson."* In the client's mind, you become irrelevant.

Options

When choosing options for inventory homes, builders primarily consider current market trends in the area, analyzing what features are most popular with potential buyers, aiming to create a home that appeals to a broad demographic while still offering some level of customization through a selection of pre-determined upgrade options, all while keeping an eye on cost-effectiveness to maximize profit margins.

Here are the key factors builders consider:

- **<u>Local market analysis</u>** – Studying local demographics, buyer preferences, and recent sales data to understand the features most in demand in that area.

- **Price point**: Balancing high-end features with affordability to attract buyers within their targeted price range.

- **Standard features vs. upgrades**: Select a base level of quality for standard features and offer optional upgrades and structural changes for buyers who want to personalize their homes.

- **Design trends** – Incorporating current design trends in aesthetics, color palettes, and layout to appeal to modern buyers.

- **Competition**—Analyzing what other builders offer to stay competitive and differentiate their inventory homes.

- **Cost efficiency** – Choosing materials and finishes that offer good value for the price while maintaining quality.

Typical options builders might offer for a feeling of customization in inventory homes include:

- **Flooring** – Different types of hardwood, tile, or carpet with varying levels of quality.

- **Countertops** – Granite, quartz, and laminate options with different color choices, thicknesses, and finishes.

- **Cabinetry** – Various styles and finishes for kitchen and bathrooms.

- **Appliances** – Different brands and models depending on price point.

- **Lighting fixtures** – Various styles and finishes for different rooms.

- **<u>Exterior finishes</u>** – Siding colors, trim details, and landscaping options.

Whether the construction supervisor accompanies you or you inspect the inventory home yourself, taking quality interior and exterior photos is crucial. The pictures you snap serve two critical purposes:

- **<u>Reminder</u>** – As you build a portfolio of builder partners, you will visit many new home communities and walk through numerous model homes and countless inventory homes. The communities and homes will have many similarities, but they will also have plenty of differences. A good way to separate builders, communities, and home designs is through good-quality photographs. These photographs will help you remember the differences between builders and their similarities. An idea worth considering is to add captions to each photo. It's time-consuming but worth it, especially when sharing photos with your clients.

- **<u>Marketing</u>** – In a survey by the National Association of Realtors, home buyers rated photos as the feature they use most when searching for a home. The quality of your images will capture the attention of current and future clients. They also form the foundation of your marketing strategy, including social media, email, text, and possibly a website.

Photography

So, how do you make a good impression with your real estate photos? What follows are things you might consider doing:

- **<u>Invest in a decent camera</u>** – A cell phone won't cut it if you want quality shots, but top-of-the-line equipment isn't necessary either. Any point-and-shoot digital camera with five megapixels or more will produce good photos. A tripod is also a good investment for taking sharp images.

- **<u>Choose the best room angle</u>** - Shooting from a corner or doorway is the best way to show off a room. Use a wide-angle lens to capture the entire room and use landscape orientation. When photographing the home's exterior, stand at an angle to the home rather than straight on. Avoid photographing objects that obscure the house, like wires or poles, as much as possible.

- **<u>Take lots of photos</u>** – Digital cameras allow you to take as many pictures as you want, so experiment with different angles and camera settings.

- **<u>Touch up the photos</u>** - After you have chosen your best photos, you will probably find that they need a bit of tweaking. Maybe the kitchen, gathering room, or bedrooms look too dark. Fortunately, free online photo editing tools like Picnik and Snipshot are easy to use and allow you to crop your pictures, adjust brightness and contrast, correct colors, and remove objects that obscure the house.

Digital Builder Binder or Photo Album

The pictures you have taken need to be downloaded to your computer. You have two choices: you can download them to your Digital Builder Binder or create a Photo Album for each house plan. Because they are JPEG or PNG files, I recommend you make a Photo Album for each builder partner. The photo album process is the same as the Digital Builder Binder. Here is an example:

- **My Builder Partner Pictures Folder**

  - **Builder Partner – (name of builder) Subfolder**

    - House Plan Pictures #1

    - House Plan Pictures #2

    - House Plan Pictures #3

    - Etc.

  - **Builder Partner – (name of builder) Subfolder**

    - House Plan Pictures #1

    - House Plan Pictures #2

    - House Plan Pictures #3

    - Etc.

<u>*PRICING*</u>

Builders price their inventory homes by calculating the total construction cost, including land, materials, labor, and overhead, which includes general and administrative expenses, marketing, compensation, and then adding a gross profit margin.

According to the National Association of Home Builders Cost of Doing Business Study, builders average a gross profit margin of 18% and a 7% net profit margin. So, a $400,000 house will gross the builder around $72,000 and net the builder $28,000.

If you discuss gross and net profit margins with your clients, use the 18% and 7% margins; I assure you that your profit numbers will be close to accurate. Don't be surprised if your clients doubt your estimates. The average new home buyer has no idea what a builder makes when constructing a new home. Invite them to Google, *New Home Builder, Gross and Net Profit Estimates*.

Knowledge of home builder profits is essential to negotiating effectively with a builder. Book Six in the series, *Negotiating with a New Home Builder*, explores the negotiating process fully.

Pricing is subject to change based on the area's current demand and inventory levels. This means a builder will adjust their inventory pricing quickly if homes in the area are selling fast (price increase) or if the house remains unsold after 60 days (price decrease). They may also provide mortgage rate buydowns and closing cost assistance to entice buyers and offer agents increased commissions rather than lowering prices.

When discussing pricing with your clients, remember that builders are reluctant to lower their base prices (a house with standard features and no options added) because it may affect future appraisals. The discounts your client may receive are linked to the upgrades the builder included in the house.

VOLUME HOME BUILDER MARKETING

Volume builders have a fully staffed marketing department to market homes. Their sole function is to set the builder apart by capturing the attention of home buyers and Realtors. Through their efforts, you are provided with the information you need when communicating the value of buying a new home versus a resale home.

So, after you have toured the house, please take a few moments to look at three sources of information provided by the builder's marketing department.

- Builder's website

- Third-party marketplace sites

- Social media

Builder Website

Most volume builders update their websites every night. Here, you will find the most up-to-date information on the home you just toured, including house description, community information, pricing, floor plan, options list, possibly a video tour, financing options, and any special promotion to entice agents to show the home.

If you haven't already done so, search for the builder online, then bookmark the site so you can return to learn more about other builder communities and inventory homes.

Third-Party Marketplace Sites

The rise of the digital world has changed everything about marketing for builders. It is not enough to have a website; the builder must have a presence everywhere, including sites like Zillow, Realtor.com, Trulia, Yahoo Real Estate, and your local MLS. In addition, a favorite site of mine is New Home Source Professional. It is an excellent source of new home information.

I encourage you to visit *newhomesourceprofessional.com* and log in via your local MLS brokerage or register as an agent. While on the site, I want you to search for the inventory home you toured. If it is listed, you should see community and home photos, a plan rendering, commission rate, client registration policies, upcoming builder events targeted toward agents and prospective home buyers, and much more.

New Home Source Professional is the go-to place for Realtors to gather new home information quickly and accurately. My only caution is that when you click on a builder or community to learn more, expect to receive a follow-up email from the builder's online sales agent. Some agents may find this annoying, but I believe it is a good opportunity to open a dialogue with the builder.

Social Media

The last source of information I want you to review is the builder's social media accounts. If you feel good about what you have experienced, follow the builder on social media. Most volume builders will be active on Facebook, Instagram, and LinkedIn. After touring the home, engage with the builder by liking, commenting, and sharing a post showcasing the community and new home designs. The goal is to get noticed by the builder.

There are many benefits to following your favorite builders on social media:

- **<u>Stay informed about new listings</u>**: Get early information about new construction projects and upcoming inventory.

- **<u>Build relationships with builders</u>**: Foster connections with key builders in your local area.

- **<u>Generate leads</u>**: Share builder updates on your social media accounts to reach potential buyers interested in new homes.

- **<u>Market expertise</u>**: Demonstrate knowledge about the local construction market to your clients.

<u>NEGOTIATING WITH A NEW HOME BUILDER</u>

When representing a client with a home to sell, you must deal with the seller's emotional attachment to the house. Fortunately, that attachment isn't part of the equation with new home builders. The home you tour is part of the builder's sales strategy. Their goal is to sell the house during construction or shortly after completion. So, every inventory house you visit is a home that should be negotiated.

The degree of price and option flexibility depends on market conditions, the construction stage, and the house's age. However, builders generally don't want to sell an inventory house at an amount lower than the asking price because doing so sets a bad precedent for future buyers and appraisers. So, how can you negotiate with a builder to get a good deal for your client? Consider negotiating for all or some of the following:

- Builder pays a share of the client's closing costs.

- A builder's preferred or owned mortgage company lowers the client's mortgage loan interest rate. The builder absorbs the cost of the buydown.

- Builder adding options that won't cause additional construction. Examples include:

  - Blinds for all windows.

  - Ceiling fans.

  - Upgrade landscaping.

  - Upgrade appliances.

  - Upgrade lighting.

  - Adding an extra gate to the backyard fence.

  - Builder paying for a third-party inspection report.

  - Etc.

The critical thing to remember here is that negotiations on inventory homes relate to more than the price. As you walk through the house, look for what has been added and other options that could be added. Think about the client who is going to live in the house. What will they need when they move into the home? Too many agents focus only on the price when they should also consider a client's after-closing needs.

Are there inventory homes where you should negotiate for a lower price? The answer is absolutely. But the house must fit one or both of the following situations:

- Aging inventory

- Location

Aging Inventory

Most volume builders construct their homes using lines of credit. As the home is constructed, the builder pays interest on the money borrowed to build the house. As the home ages, the cost of the home increases not only through interest charges but also through maintenance. Those two factors motivate the builder to negotiate options and pricing. The older the house, the more motivated the builder is. I encourage you to learn the age of every inventory home; if the home has been completed for sixty days or more, negotiate for a lower price and any options to improve your client's after-closing experience.

Location

When builders construct a house on a challenging lot, they are prepared to negotiate with both options and pricing. So, when you walk through an inventory home, look at the house through the eyes of a buyer. Is there anything you see that your clients will object to? If you can recognize the challenge, so won't your clients. Please take pictures of the challenge and include them in your notes.

NEW HOME NEGOTIATION PROCEDURES

To my surprise, many of the agents I have trained are surprised that builders are willing to negotiate on price (under certain conditions) and options. When I explain the three situations a builder bases his decision on, it is like a light bulb goes off in their head. They begin to see how successfully negotiating with a builder is possible. Those three conditions are:

1. House to be built.

2. House under construction.

3. Completed house.

What follows are the procedures most volume builders follow regarding new home negotiations.

House To Be Built

Builders are reluctant to negotiate on a home built from the ground up. They reason that material, labor, and finance costs may increase during construction. Does this mean a builder won't negotiate? No, everything is negotiable, and builders understand that their competitors will if they don't negotiate. So, most volume builders will add a dollar amount to the housing budget for negotiating. The amount will depend on whether the builder is experiencing a seller's or buyer's market. In addition to the dollar amount in the budget, builders will offer your clients an incentive if they use their preferred or owned mortgage and title company.

Houses Under Construction

All builders aim to sell their inventory houses during construction or within sixty days of completion. For that reason, homes under construction offer your client a realistic opportunity to negotiate. However, the possibility of adding options diminishes as the house moves from one construction phase to another. A typical volume builder will stick to the following schedule:

Phase Three – Lot Benched

- Structural changes.

- Plumbing rough changes.

- Fireplace addition.

- Under slab electrical changes.

Phase Three – Slab Complete

- Upgrade to kitchen and bathroom cabinets.

- Upgrade to mechanicals.

- Adding low voltage wiring.

- Upgrading or changing garage door.

- Upgrading or changing exterior door.

- Upgrading insulation package.

- Changing paint and trim colors on the interior and exterior.

- Upgrading stair style.

Phase Six – Drywall complete

- Flooring.

- Countertops.

- Plumbing fixtures.

- Lighting fixtures.

- Flatwork.

- Fencing.

- Door hardware.

The following may be added anytime during construction:

- Refrigerator.

- Washer and dryer.

- Window blinds.

- Garage door opener.

As you see, purchasing an inventory home under construction offers your clients an excellent opportunity to personalize the home to their tastes. It also provides the opportunity to utilize the incentive money a builder offers when your clients choose to use a builder's preferred or owned mortgage and title company.

In addition to the incentive money, you can negotiate for additional options because the builder has included a dollar amount in their budget. Please note that the builder will not negotiate the house price while the home is under construction, so the focus of negotiation should be on options.

The options your client can add depend on the phase of construction and the building products that have already been ordered. So, if your client likes the house and wants to personalize it, remind them that time is of the essence. Builders have a construction schedule to keep and will not wait for your client. As each day passes, the opportunity to add options decreases.

Completed Home

If a builder has a home ready to move into, builders are more inclined typically to lower the price, as this helps them avoid carrying the house's expenses. Don't be shy about negotiating a deep discount on the price, especially if the home has been completed for over sixty days.

The time of the year can significantly impact your negotiating ability for a lower price. Here is what you need to know:

Seasonal fluctuations:

- Spring and fall are typically the busiest sales times of the year. During those months, you might face more competition and higher prices.

- Slower periods typically occur during winter and late summer months. These low-demand periods can be perfect for finding good deals, as builders are more willing to negotiate to move unsold inventory.

- The school year impacts demand because many families prefer to move during summer break to avoid disrupting their children's education.

End-of-year or end-of-quarter opportunities:

- Most volume builders are more willing to negotiate on price near the end of their fiscal or calendar year. They are pressured to boost sales numbers or clear aging inventory before a new financial period begins.

- Volume builders observing a calendar year refer to twelve consecutive months, beginning January 1 and ending December 31. Builders who observe a fiscal year mean twelve consecutive months ending on the last day of any month except December.

- All volume builders have established quarterly sales goals. The pressure to reach their sales targets makes them much more receptive to deals, especially if they are experiencing slower-than-expected sales.

Builder Bonuses:

- All volume builders offer their management team bonuses. A bonus payment is given at the end of the year (calendar or fiscal) or can be awarded monthly or quarterly. The bonus is typically based on the company's overall profitability, individual community performance, or a combination of these elements. The one thing all bonuses have in common is sales. Sales are what drive profit. Profit is what drives bonuses. The better the sales performance, the better the bonus is for each management team member.

Never forget that negotiating is not personal for the builder, but a business matter. So, don't be shy about finding out if your chosen builder partners observe a fiscal or calendar year for accounting purposes. The benefit to you is an increase in sales and income, and a lower price or additional options for your clients.

Chapter Twelve Key Takeaways

Chapter Twelve provides an overview of the key aspects you need to know to choose the right volume builder for you and your clients. To reinforce your understanding of the material in this chapter, take a few minutes to answer the following three questions? Answering these key takeaways will strengthen your understanding of the chapter's main ideas and aid your ongoing learning about working and partnering with the new home builder community.

1. What spoke to you most about this chapter?

2. What insight in these pages made the most significant impression on you?

3. How will you take what you have learned in this chapter, and put it into action in your pursuit of new home sales?

Selecting the Right Salesperson for You and Your Clients

WHAT SHOULD A NEW home buyer expect when visiting a builder's model home for the first time? They should anticipate a fully furnished and decorated house showcasing the different floor plans and design options available, with a sales representative on-site to guide them through the tour and answer their questions about homes, homesites, location, community, financing, and the builder while allowing them to experience the feel of living in that home. They should be prepared to discuss their needs, budget, and preferred features to help narrow their choices.

When you visit the model home sales center for the first time, be prepared to be a homebuyer, not a real estate agent. As a prospective homebuyer, you will experience what your clients should expect when interacting with the on-site salesperson. This interaction will be the final step in selecting a builder you can, without reservation, refer to your clients and a builder you can partner with.

What follows is a step-by-step guide for that first visit. As I mentioned, some of you reading this book may be skeptical of my suggestion. However, if you do what I recommend, the information you gather will be the difference that helps you build your new home sales business.

BE A SECRET SHOPPER

You are probably familiar with the term secret shopper. The idea of being shopped secretly may turn you off. You may feel it is an invasion of your privacy. But for a moment, please remove your Realtor hat and become the builder's sales manager.

As the sales manager, you are responsible for the performance of your sales team. You have trained them to greet customers respectfully, qualify for needs and wants, build value in different home designs by focusing on features and benefits, overcome objections, and close the sale. But how do you know they are using the selling skills you taught them? The quick answer is, "*You don't.*" Unless you employ the services of a mystery shopper, posing as a regular customer to evaluate the quality of their sales presentation.

Most volume builders believe that what you measure, you improve. Since new home salespeople work alone or partner with another salesperson, builders cannot measure their selling skills other than through a secret shopper. I advise you to become a secret shopper to learn how your clients will be treated during and after meeting with the builder's on-site salesperson.

Secret Shopper Guidelines

To become a convincing secret shopper, follow these guidelines to make your mystery shop more believable.

- Develop a backstory to support your role as a secret shopper.

- Write and commit to memory your visit expectations.

- Allow the on-site salesperson to present the home with features and benefits without interruption.

- If asked questions about your current situation, answer them.

- If asked for a phone number, provide it.

- If followed up by the on-site salesperson, respond promptly.

- Take photos (ask for permission first).

- File notes following completion of sales presentation.

The succeeding section explores each of the guidelines.

Secret Shopper Backstory

A secret shopper's backstory refers to the fictional narrative a mystery shopper creates about themselves when posing as a regular customer. Your story should include details about your housing needs, your shopping experience for both new and resale homes, and the reason for visiting the model home. In addition, you must be prepared to answer the salesperson's qualifying questions.

A qualifying question uncovers all the personal information a salesperson needs to know about you. What follows are the qualifying questions you can expect:

- **<u>Your visit motivation</u>**: The reason you are visiting the model home.

- **<u>Where you are presently living</u>**: The location of your current residence.

- **<u>Your living situation</u>**: Are you single, married, with or without children?

- **<u>Own or rent</u>**: Do you own a house or are you renting? If you rent, how many months remain on the lease?

- **<u>Employment</u>**: Where you are currently working and for how long.

- **<u>Timing and urgency</u>**: What is your time frame for purchasing and moving?

- **<u>Shopping experience</u>**: Are you considering other housing alternatives (e.g., resale, renting, staying put, or another new home builder)?

- **<u>Price range</u>**: How much house can you afford?

- **<u>Income</u>**: The amount of income available to satisfy monthly mortgage payments.

- **<u>Initial investment or earnest money</u>**: The money you currently have available to secure the house until the mortgage is approved.

- **<u>Debt</u>**: The percentage of your monthly income assigned to current monthly obligations.

The most important part of a backstory is answering the salesperson's qualifying questions. Here is an example of a typical exchange with an experienced salesperson, where you respond to their qualifying questions.

Backstory Example

Salesperson: *"What are you looking for in a home?"*

You: *"Well, I'm not sure. We've just started looking. We need four bedrooms because we're expecting our third child this fall and require more space. We also need a larger family room; if possible, we want separate closets in our bedroom."*

Salesperson: *"I understand. You mentioned you have just started looking. Are we the first builder you have looked at?"*

You: *"No, we toured two other home builders and several resale homes, but nothing we saw is what we are looking for."*

Salesperson: *"I am confident we can find what you want here. You mentioned that you are expecting your third child. To confirm, is anyone else besides yourself, your husband, and the children who will live in the home with you?"*

You: *"Possibly my mother. She might move in with us, but that decision has not yet been made. It will be the five of us right now."*

Salesperson: *"Thanks for sharing that information. It helps me understand your family situation. Is there anything else besides the four bedrooms, a larger family room, and, if possible, separate closets in your bedroom?"*

You: *"Not that I can think of. Well, maybe, if we can afford it, we would like to have a three-car garage. My husband's brother recently purchased a home with a three-car garage, and he and his wife like having the extra storage space."*

Salesperson: *"You mentioned affordability. Do you have a price range in mind?"*

You: *"Not really. We know we don't want our monthly payments to exceed $3000."*

Salesperson: *"I am sure that is possible. One last financial thing to cover is earnest money. Do you have funds to secure the home through mortgage approval?"*

You: *"That depends on what you require. We have been saving for about a year, and my husband is expecting a year-end bonus."*

Salesperson: *"We require $1000 at contract signing and an additional five percent before the start of construction. You can use either conventional or FHA financing. If you have time today, I will show you the benefits of both plans. Is there anything else besides four bedrooms, a larger family room, separate closets, and, if possible, a third-car garage?"*

You: *"Let me think; I'm sure there's something else I'm missing, but I believe that covers the things my husband and I discussed."*

Now, let's examine the information the salesperson has acquired by asking qualifying questions.

Shopping Experience

The salesperson learned you are considering new and resale homes. They discovered you visited two other home builders but did not identify either builder by name. You should expect the salesperson to ask a follow-up question to learn who the other two builders were. Additionally, expect the salesperson to ask what you were looking for, which neither builder offered.

Your Living Situation

The salesperson learned you are expecting a third child in the fall, which led the salesperson to ask about who else will live in the home with you. The salesperson discovered that your mother may live with you in addition to your husband and three children, but that decision has not been finalized. Expect the salesperson to ask a follow-up question about whether a home with a mother-in-law suite should be considered.

Price Range

The salesperson asked if you had a price range in mind, and you answered by providing a monthly mortgage payment instead. This distinction is essential to understand. Most new home buyers think about what they can afford monthly, not the price range. While this is true, it is not helpful to the salesperson. Expect the salesperson to explore a price range further, as they want to eliminate homes that are above what you can afford.

Initial Investment or Earnest Money

The salesperson transitioned from discussing the price range to the funds required to hold the house through mortgage approval and then to the funds needed for the start of construction. You provided an answer that will require a follow-up question to confirm that you have the necessary funds to secure the house. The salesperson then transitioned you into the builder's different financing programs. Prepare yourself to avoid further discussion about financing until you tour the home and see if what the builder is offering is what you and your husband have in mind.

Housing Needs

The salesperson asked what you wanted in a home. You answered four bedrooms, separate closets, and a larger family room. Expect the salesperson to ask additional questions about your housing needs. In the exchange example, the salesperson asked, *"Is there anything else?"* You responded, *"A three-car garage if we can afford it."*

Preparation is the Key

All this information was obtained in a brief conversation because the salesperson knew precisely what to ask and listen for. That is why, as a secret shopper, you should prepare yourself for an experienced and knowledgeable salesperson.

I know that most new home salespeople will not be as professional as the salesperson in the example. But you won't know their experience level until you shop with them. To be prudent, you must prepare for a curious and skillful salesperson.

Preparation is the key to a successful secret shopper. Be prepared to answer qualifying questions and follow-up questions. The advantage of preparing to be a mystery shopper is that it only needs to be done once, and can be adjusted to fit other builders you mystery shop.

Set Visit Expectations

Throughout this book, I have referenced setting expectations but have not fully explained their value to your success. You relinquish the buying process to the builder's salesperson without setting expectations. By establishing visit expectations, you can successfully achieve the outcome you have in mind while maintaining a high level of rapport with the builder's on-site agent and positioning yourself apart from other real estate agents.

To set expectations with the on-site salesperson, you must do the following:

- Clearly and openly communicate your needs and desired outcomes.

- Identify precisely what you want to accomplish during the model home tour.

- Ensure the salesperson understands what is expected of them while being realistic and open to compromise.

Here is a visit expectation example that clearly defines what you want from the on-site salesperson:

***

My purpose for today's visit is to learn about the community and the builder, and familiarize myself with your homes. Would you be available to answer my questions and walk me through the model

home today, pointing out what makes your homes different from those of other home builders?

***

Let's examine why this example sets the visit expectation that allows you to control the buying process while maintaining rapport and professionalism with the on-site salesperson.

- You immediately established your purpose for today's visit. When the salesperson understands why you are there, they can help you achieve what you want.

- You established that you want to learn about the community and builder, and familiarize yourself with the builder's homes. You also stated that you want to know what makes their homes different from other home builders. This informs the salesperson that you know what you want.

- You did not assume the salesperson's availability. This lets the salesperson know you respect their time and will be flexible if they have other commitments today.

When you set expectations, you create a visit roadmap for you and the on-site salesperson to follow. When the salesperson agrees with your purpose, they have acknowledged that they will help you achieve your visit goals. If the salesperson wanders away from your objectives, you can gently pull them back in your desired direction.

During a model home visit, you can choose to be in control or to be controlled. When you set visit expectations, you are in charge. I hope you see the benefit and will prepare yourself to take the lead.

Here are two brief scenarios, one in which the salesperson takes control and the other in which you seize control.

Scenario #1

Salesperson: *"Greetings, how may I help you today?"*

You: *"I am just looking."*

Salesperson: *"Sure, but before we start, would you mind answering just one question?"*

You: *"Okay, what is your question?"*

Salesperson: *"What brought you to my model home today?"*

Stop reading for a moment, and, in your mind, ask yourself how you would answer that question. Suppose you answered it by saying, *"I've driven by here several times and was curious to see the type of homes you are building here"*. Or you responded, *"My husband and I are considering moving, but we are unsure whether we should purchase an existing home or buy a new one."*

Now, ask yourself this question: *"**Who is in control?**"* The answer is the salesperson. To make my point, let's return to your exchange with the salesperson to find out where the salesperson goes next.

You: *"My husband and I are considering moving, but we are unsure whether we should purchase an existing home or buy a new one."*

Salesperson: *"You mentioned moving. Is this something you are considering doing now?"*

Once again, stop reading and consider what the salesperson is doing. The salesperson has taken control of the buying process by asking you qualifying questions. This is what new home salespeople are taught to do. They use qualifying questions to uncover all the personal information they need to know about you.

The answer you provided opened many different possibilities, including:

- Your reason for visiting the model home.

- Your living situation.

- Whether you own or rent.

- Timing and urgency.

- Shopping experience.

- Price range.

Salespeople are taught to listen for trigger words in your response, allowing them to transition into things they need to know about you. The trigger words in your response included *"husband, moving, used home, and new home."*

The word *"husband"* allows the salesperson to transition to your living situation, timing, and urgency. The word *"moving"* enables the salesperson to transition to where you live, whether you own or rent, and your desired price range. The words *"used" and "new home "* allow the salesperson to transition into your shopping experience.

Remember, this exchange began with a simple question by the salesperson, *"Greetings, how may I help you today?"* Because the salesperson was experienced and knew how to ask qualifying questions, they could take control of the sales presentation. You must assume all salespeople are experienced in asking need-to-know questions and prepare to manage the buying process by setting visit expectations that allow you to be in charge.

Let's examine how to redirect the sales presentation by adding your visit expectations, while maintaining rapport with the salesperson.

Scenario #2

Salesperson: *"Greetings, how may I help you today?"*

You: *"My husband and I are considering moving, but we are unsure whether to purchase another existing home or buy a new one. So, my purpose today is to learn about your community and the builder, and familiarize myself with your homes. Would you be available to answer my questions and walk me through the model home today, pointing out what makes your homes different from other home builders?"*

Salesperson: *"I can answer questions about the community and builder, and have time before my next appointment to walk through the model home. Let's start with a community overview."*

As you can see from that exchange, setting clear visit expectations makes it easy to direct the sales presentation where you want it to go. Even though you are in control, you should expect the salesperson to sprinkle in qualifying questions throughout the sales presentation while answering your questions about the community, the builder, and what makes their homes unique compared to the competition.

Your sales presentation goal is to have a conversation with the salesperson. This way, you secure the information you need to make an informed decision, and the salesperson captures what they need to know about you. When you set visit expectations, you lay the foundation for a two-way conversation that allows you and the salesperson to move toward what you both want: the sale and purchase of a new home.

Before moving on to the next step in becoming a believable secret shopper, I would like to discuss the importance of incorporating a life-changing event into your backstory. This discussion will teach you a valuable lesson that will change the way you look at and understand what motivates your clients.

Life-Change

A home search begins when a life-changing event motivates someone to seek different housing options. The event may be marriage, the birth of a child, a new job, a job promotion, relocation, a child's graduation, divorce or separation, inheritance, retirement, empty nesting, or the death of a loved one. The point is that these life-changing events cause people to examine their current housing situation.

When a life-changing event is about to occur or has occurred, they start questioning whether they should look for new housing or stay put. Individuals or families begin to consider whether more or less space is required, whether they can afford a larger home due to an increase in disposable income, or, in the case of job promotion and relocation, whether they are motivated to buy and sell because they have no choice.

Everyone has experienced life-changing events. I have moved twelve times in my life. Most of my moves were caused by job promotions. However, my last move was family-motivated. I was 55 years old; two of my four children had married and were starting their own families. I was busy traveling throughout the country, doing sales training seminars for builders. I spent three to four days a week flying here and there, and when I was home, I was busy preparing for the next trip. I was leading a fast-paced life. And then everything changed in an instant.

I began to notice changes; my breathing was labored, and I tired quickly. My body was telling me something was wrong. Then, one Sunday after-noon in June 2000, walking back from a church festival, I had an angina attack. Angina occurs when the heart has to work harder because the supply of oxygen is inadequate to meet the needs of the heart muscle.

The next day, I contacted my doctor. I explained my symptoms. To be safe, he suggested performing some tests. He instructed me to go to the hospital, and he would meet me there. Following an EKG and stress test, I was told I had serious heart issues.

I was admitted to the hospital and, within twenty-four hours, was lying on an operating table undergoing angioplasty. Unfortunately for me, I had two major artery blocks (the doctor referred to them as widow makers) and a heart valve that was regurgitating fifty percent of my blood flow back into my heart. Due to the location of the artery blocks and my leaking heart valve, angioplasty was not an option. The next day, I had open-heart surgery. In an instant, my life had changed, and with that, my priorities.

During my three months of recovery, my wife and I evaluated our lives and decided that traveling and being away from the family was not how I should live the rest of my life. We decided that I would give up touring and training. We moved to Texas to be closer to our children and grandchildren. This life-changing experience was the motivating factor that led us to purchase the home we are currently living in.

I share this story with you so that you understand the importance of life-changing events in deciding whether to purchase a home. If I didn't have heart problems, I would most likely still be living in Cincinnati, Ohio. We only considered moving to Texas after my heart issues. And so it is with people considering moving from their current living situation. Rest assured, there will always be a reason connected to life that motivates people to move.

Secret Shopper Backstory Continued

I am confident you know what I will say next, but it is worth telling—moving is not easy. It is hard work. It is not something people do without a lot of thought and consideration. People must be motivated to move from their present situation to a new one. You need to understand this motivation; motivation is what separates serious buyers from curious lookers.

Motivation is the catalyst that causes someone to visit an open house or a builder's model home. Therefore, the first step in becoming a secret shopper is incorporating your buying motivation into your backstory.

In Scenario # 2, you answered the salesperson's greeting: *"My husband and I are considering moving, but we are unsure whether to purchase another existing home or buy a new one."* With this response, did you provide the salesperson with your motivation? No, you did not. You explained you were considering moving but were unsure whether to buy another existing home or a new one. So, you should expect the salesperson to follow up and ask additional questions about why you are considering moving.

Buying Motivations

There are four primary buying motivations:

1. Family.

2. Investment.

3. Convenience.

4. Prestige.

So, as you build your secret shopper's backstory, consider which buying motivation(s) caused you to purchase your last home. Did you buy the house for family reasons? Were you moving from a smaller home to a more spacious one because a larger home will provide the convenience you lacked in your existing home? Were you moving to a new location because it offered your family an investment opportunity and prestige?

Remember, each client you work with will be motivated according to their needs, wants, and what is important to them. My wife and I moved to Texas to be closer to family. Additionally, my wife wanted the convenience of a swimming pool so the grandchildren could learn to swim and the whole family could enjoy time together. In addition to my wife's motivation, I wanted a location that would retain its value and build equity over time.

Our motivations represented the conditions under which we made our decisions. If our Realtor showed us a property without a pool or one that wasn't located in an area where the property would appreciate, we would say, "*Not for us,*" and move on to another home that met or exceeded our decision-making criteria. With the help of our Realtor, we found the right home for us.

Now, consider what motivated you to buy or lease your first, second, or third home. Were you motivated to move because of family, investment, convenience, or prestige? What moved you to accept the challenge of changing your living situation? Once you have your motivations in mind, please write them down. Your motivations are the heart of your backstory.

To summarize, I provided the following exchange earlier. As you read it, see if you can identify your motivations and the salesperson's follow-up qualifying questions. If you can do it, you understand buying motivation and qualifying questions.

Salesperson: *"Thanks for sharing that information. It helps me understand your family situation. Is there anything else besides the four bedrooms, a larger family room, and, if possible, separate closets in your bedroom?"*

You: *"Not that I can think of. Well, maybe, if we can afford it, we would like to have a three-car garage. My husband's brother recently purchased a home with a three-car garage, and he and his wife like having the extra storage space."*

Salesperson: *"You mentioned affordability. Do you have a price range in mind?"*

You: *"Not really. We know we don't want our monthly payments to exceed $3000."*

Salesperson: *"I am sure that is possible. One last financial thing to cover is earnest money. Do you have funds to secure the home through mortgage approval?"*

You: *"That depends on what you require. We have been saving for about a year, and my husband is expecting a year-end bonus."*

What follows are the motivations and qualifying questions included in this brief exchange between you and the salesperson.

Your Motivations

Motivations – The reasons you are considering changing your living situation.

- **Family**

  - You stated you wanted four bedrooms, a larger family room because of a growing family.

- **Convenience**

  - Separate closets in your bedroom.

- **Investment**

  - You stated you did not want the monthly payment to exceed $3000 dollars.

  - You stated that a third-car garage would be nice for extra storage if you could afford it.

Salesperson's Qualifying Questions

- The salesperson asked, "*Is there anything else?*"

  - You responded with a three-car garage for extra storage. if it is affordable.

- The salesperson repeated your word *"Affordability"* to learn about your price range.

  - You responded that you did not want the monthly payment to exceed $3000.

- The salesperson transitioned from affordability to earnest money.

  - You responded that it depends. We have been saving for a year, and my husband expects a year-end bonus.

SECRET SHOPPER SUMMARY

Hopefully, you are beginning to understand what needs to happen to become a successful secret shopper. It takes thought and preparation. But as I have written, you only have to create one backstory and be able to answer the salesperson's need-to-know qualifying questions. What follows is a summary of what you have been asked to do to develop a believable backstory.

Write out a paragraph or two that represents your real-life story. Include your motivations and the reasons that drove you to change your living situation. Was it family, convenience, investment, or prestige?

Develop answers to the salesperson's qualifying questions. Use your personal experiences to answer the questions. Here are the things the salesperson is likely to ask you questions about:

- What is your visit motivation?

- Where are you presently living?

- What is your current living situation (are you married, single, children)?

- Do you own or rent?

- What is your employment status?

- What is your timing and urgency for moving?

- What is your shopping experience?

- Do you have a price range in mind?

- What is your income?

- Do you have funds to secure the house and earnest money to begin construction?

- What is your debt status?

Write out your visit expectations so you control the buying process. Here is an example:

***

My purpose for today's visit is to learn about the community and the builder, and familiarize myself with your homes. Would you be available to answer my questions and walk me through the model home today, pointing out what makes your homes different from those of other home builders?"

***

I know what I am asking you to do is not easy. It will take time and effort, but I promise the return on your investment will outweigh the cost. Remember this idea: success comes to those willing to do what others are unwilling to do.

You have established your visit expectations and may have answered a few qualifying questions; now, it is time to experience the model home.

MODEL HOME SALES PRESENTATION

Demonstrating the model home is an essential part of the salesperson's responsibilities. Your role as a secret shopper is to participate in the process. For that to occur, I believe it is helpful to understand what the salesperson is attempting to achieve. What follows are five things the salesperson wants to make happen:

- To establish their credibility through product knowledge.

- To sell the builder's advantages and its reputation for quality construction.

- To explain the standard features included in the base price and point out options, structural changes, and designer items unavailable for purchase.

- To ask any remaining qualifying questions and, if not already done so, ask discovery questions to understand your needs, wants, and what is important to you in a new home.

- To lead you to minor decisions by utilizing tie-down and trial-close questions.

For clarity, not every salesperson you meet has the skill or desire to execute the bullet points identified above. Most of the salespeople you meet are comfortable allowing you to walk through the model home unattended; however, that will not work for your purposes. You need to understand what makes this builder different from any other builder. And that means a model home sales presentation.

This is why setting the visit expectation is so important. By establishing the purpose of your visit, you are clearly communicating to the salesperson why you are there. You are telling the salesperson you want to know what makes the builder different from their competitors. You are telling the salesperson your purpose is to learn about the community and builder, which cannot happen without the salesperson's involvement. Finally, your visit expectation does not assume the salesperson's availability.

Let's examine the availability of on-site salespeople so you understand what is necessary to ensure you speak to the salesperson, not the salesperson's assistant.

On-Site Salesperson's Availability

On average, new home salespeople work a five-day workweek. The hours will vary by builder, but most model homes open at 10AM and close at 6PM or 7PM. Days off may also differ depending on the builder and the number of salespeople working in the model home. Typically, salespeople's days off fluctuate between Tuesday and Wednesday or Wednesday and Thursday. Most new home salespeople will be in the model home on Monday, Friday, Saturday, and Sunday.

Suppose the community you are researching is in a Master Planned Community or is a community with several builders; in that case, there will likely be two or three salespeople working on-site. Your chances of talking to a salesperson are good. However, in larger communities, you may be screened by a sales assistant before you meet with the salesperson. If this happens, no worries.

The purpose of the sales assistant is to ask you qualifying questions. Those questions will be included on a registration form. Complete the registration form accurately using your backstory as your guide. If the sales assistant asks you what you want in a new home, answer those questions. If the sales assistant offers to walk you through the model, that is where you need to draw the line. Remember, your purpose is to learn more about the community and builder, but also whether the salesperson is someone you can refer confidently to your clients.

Schedule An Appointment

My recommendation is to schedule an appointment rather than show up unannounced. I have three reasons for making this suggestion:

1. You will learn if the salesperson works alone or is partnered with other salespeople.

2. You will learn if the salesperson has a full-time assistant who may or may not be your only contact until you meet with the salesperson.

3. You will learn the salesperson's weekly schedule, including days off and hours at the model home.

Everything identified above is essential information and should be included in your Digital Builder Binder under the builder's name and community.

I don't want you to waste your valuable time. Take the time to phone the office; I promise it will be a call that enables you to be more productive in the limited time you have to build your new home sales business.

On-Site Salespeople's Model Home Partnership

Before moving on to the actual phone call and how it should be done, I want you to understand the partnership between salespeople and how it might affect you. When more than one salesperson manages sales in the model home, they typically have a partnership agreement that involves sharing home buyers and compensation. I see this working relationship as a plus for you. Here are my reasons:

1. A salesperson is always available in the model home to assist with your client's buying situation.

2. When your client has a construction issue, they can discuss it with a salesperson who knows them and wants to solve whatever problem they have identified.

3. Communication between your client, the builder, and the on-site salespeople will be better because they have a team working with them on your behalf. One of the biggest complaints new home buyers have about working with builders is a lack of communication. Partnerships between salespeople, construction supervisors, and the builder's office personnel can significantly reduce communication issues.

The Phone Call

Careful planning is essential to placing a phone call to secure an appointment with a full-time salesperson. Before you pick up the phone, ask yourself if you are clear about your objectives. For this first phone call, please write down those objectives and keep them in front of you. Examples of phone call objectives include:

- Your name and the purpose of your call (what you want).

- Salesperson or salespeople's names with correct spelling and pronunciation.

- Sales Assistant's name with correct spelling and pronunciation.

- Model home hours of operation.

- Salesperson or salespeople's days off.

A good way to stay in control of the phone call is to follow a well-planned, not canned, presentation. Here are the ingredients of a well-planned phone call:

Phone Call Example

Identification

Identify yourself (your name) and the reason for this phone call.

You: *Hi, this is (your name). I drove through your community on (whatever day you visited the community). I am calling to learn more about the community and the builder. To whom am I speaking?*

Qualify for the Model Home Position

If the response only includes the name and not their position, you must ask for clarification about their role in the model home.

You: *Thank you (their name). Are you the salesperson for (community)?*

Sales Assistant: *I am not the salesperson; I assist (salesperson's name) on her days off.*

Phone Call Objective

Remember that you aim to schedule an appointment with the full-time salesperson. Therefore, if the answer is *"Sales Assistant,"* that is of no concern; continue with the following response.

You: *As I mentioned, I drove through the community (whatever day you visited) and want to schedule an appointment with the salesperson to learn more about the community and builder. Can I schedule an appointment with you to talk with the salesperson.*

Sales Assistant: *Sure, I can schedule it for tomorrow. (Salesperson's name) arrives at ten. Do you have a time when you would like to meet?*

Or

Sales Assistant: *(Salesperson's name) will be out of the office until Friday; I can meet with you tomorrow. I am sure I can answer your questions.*

Schedule an Appointment

Ask for what you want, which is an appointment with the salesperson. Remember your objective: Is this a salesperson I will feel comfortable referring to my clients? Your response may sound something like this.

You: Well, if it's okay with you, I'd rather wait to talk with the salesperson on Friday. Can you schedule an appointment? I am open most of the day, so anytime in the morning or early afternoon will work well for me.

Qualify for Convenience

The question you asked to schedule an appointment is called a direct question. The only way to answer it is to tell when the salesperson will return to the office.

Sales Assistant: Yes, I can schedule a meeting on Friday. Does 11AM work for you?

Confirm and Hang Up

Don't waste time with small talk. Once you have met your objectives, end the phone call.

You: Yes, 11AM works well for me. I appreciate your help. If there's any change, please call and let me know. My name is (your name), and my phone number is (your number).

While this example focused on the sales assistant, the ingredients of the call remain the same if you are talking with the salesperson. Whether you adopt this exact format is beside the point; the goal is to adopt some planned presentation that allows you to schedule an appointment with the right person on a day and time that is convenient for you.

Ask For What You Want

I know I have said this same thing before, but I believe it bears repeating: *"In life, you get what you ask for, so ask for what you want."* My experience with new home salespeople and real estate agents is that they don't know what they want, so they settle for what is given to them. To build a new home sales business, you must understand what you want and ask for it confidently.

Throughout my career, I have been invited to speak at several National Home Builder Association (NAHB) conventions. During my presentation, I would ask the audience, *"When you meet a new client for the first time, what do you want from the experience?"* I was always surprised that very few people who volunteered a response knew precisely what they wanted. I believe this phenomenon is true of most people. But it doesn't have to be that way. If you only take the time to establish clear objectives before engaging with another person, you will find that most of the time, you get what you want.

The phone call is a perfect example of achieving what you want if you take the time to identify your objectives and write them down so you have a reminder to keep you focused.

<u>Not All Salespeople Are The Same</u>

The next step in deciding whether this is the right community and builder for your clients is evaluating the on-site salesperson. Through experience, I have determined that new home salespeople can be best described as either Participators or Administrators. Some salespeople you encounter will want to participate in touring the model home with you, while others are comfortable allowing you to tour the house alone.

I refer to the salesperson who wishes to accompany you as a Participator and the salesperson willing to let you view the model home unaccompanied as an Administrator.

Through their actions, Participators communicate that they will be active in your client's home-buying decision. In most situations, you will want this behavior from the on-site salesperson.

On the other hand, through their actions, an Administrator communicates that your client must take control of the sales and buying process by asking questions to determine the value of the community, location, homes, homesites, financing programs, and the builder. This situation is unfavorable because most people who purchase new homes are unfamiliar with the purchasing, mortgage, construction, closing, and service processes. They need help navigating through all the decisions that need to be made.

The Participator and Administrator communicate who they are and what your clients can expect. I know you want the best for your clients; just be aware of the salesperson's actions; actions usually speak louder than words.

Information the Salesperson Should Know

Sales managers are essential members of the volume builder's staff. They are responsible for training and motivating the sales team and onboarding new salespeople with the information they need about the community and the builder.

Additionally, most volume builders have annual contracts with new home sales training experts. These trainers develop builder-specific sales manuals and conduct monthly, quarterly, and yearly training sessions with the sales staff.

I speak from experience because I provided sales and marketing training to over one hundred local and national volume builders for fourteen years. Almost all my training centered on teaching the salespeople how to provide builder and community information that sets the salesperson, the builder, and the community apart from the competition.

What follows is what the on-site salesperson is taught by either a sales trainer, a sales manager, or a mentor assigned to them, but it is not always what you will experience. Suppose the information I identify below is not provided during the first visit. In that case, I recommend that you or your client ask about it at some point during the home-buying process, as everything listed is essential information your client needs to make an informed home-buying decision.

Builder:

- The builder's length of time in business.

- Their financial strength.

- The number of homes they build annually.

- Their warranty and service policies and procedures.

- Their quality inspection process during construction.

- Are they managed locally or nationally?

- Awards they have received for unique home styles and designs.

- Awards they have received for outstanding home buyer customer after-sales service.

- Average administrative time before the start of construction,

- Average builder time from the start of construction.

- Builder-owned or preferred title and mortgage company.

- Incentives connected to the title and mortgage company usage.

Builder Policies and Procedures:

- Sales contracts and addenda.

- How much earnest money is required to hold a home through mortgage approval?

- Lot hold cost and length of hold.

- Start-of-construction deposit.

- Construction start times.

- Construction changes following the start of construction.

- Construction problem reporting.

- Home buyer communications with builder partners (mortgage and title company) and in-office personnel

- Fair housing policy.

- Contract contingency

- Cancellation policy and return of earnest and start of construction deposits.

<u>Location</u>:

- Information on private and public schools.

- School proximity to the community.

- School national test scores.

- Principal's name, class sizes, school phone numbers, school facilities, and the name of the PTA president.

- Information about services located close to the community, including shopping, police and fire departments, public transportation, proximity to major highways, and recreation areas.

- Up-to-date information about county taxes and the average cost of utilities, including gas, sewer, water, and electricity.

<u>Community</u>:

- Number of houses to be built in the community.

- Houses sold to date

- Number of inventory houses available for sale and their stages of construction.

- Home buyer and Realtor incentives on inventory homes.

- Plans for future development of additional homesites.

- Is the community located in a PID or Mud District?

- Zoning for vacant land adjoining the community.

<u>Homes and Options</u>:

- The square footage of each house available for sale in the community, including the garage.

- The square footage of the living space of each available floor plan.

- The square footage of each room in the house plan.

- The options and structural upgrades available per house and homesite combination.

- Standard feature list per plan.

- House prices per plan.

- The itemized cost of homeownership per plan (principal, interest, taxes, insurance (PITI).

<u>Homesites</u>:

- The size of each homesite, acceptable house plans, and options per site.

- Location of the building envelope of each available house plan.

- Lot easements and their locations.

- Compass directions for sun orientation per homesite.

- Driveway location per homesite (right, left, side, or rear).

- Lot premiums per homesite.

- Precise dimensions per homesite.

- Tree inventory per homesite.

<u>Financing</u>:

- The different financing programs available and their current rates.

- Qualifying criteria for each finance program.

- The debt and income ratios for each financing program.

- Approval times for the underwriting application.

- How a prospective home buyer can repair credit flaws.

<u>Competition</u>:

- House designs and floor plans, prices.

- Available finance programs, rates, and qualifying criteria.

- Individual house plan prices.

- Available options and structural upgrade costs.

- Standard house features per plan.

- Price per square foot per plan.

- The quality of homesites and dimensions.

- Build and administrative times.

- Incentives to purchase.

- Realtor commissions and bonuses.

The information listed above is extensive, so don't expect the salesperson to share everything about the builder, the community, the location, and financing programs with your client on a first visit. Because you are secretly shopping the salesperson, all the above information is unnecessary. You learned a lot about the builder and community when researching the builder's website, talking with agents who are familiar with the builder and may have sold their homes, touring the community, and walking through homes under construction and finished inventory homes. I want your emphasis on this first visit to be evaluating the salesperson, so I want you to focus on securing the following information:

- Model home standard features.

- Any options or structural upgrades included in the model home?

- Designer upgrades that are visible in the model home but unavailable for purchase.

- Inventory or spec home availability and the status of construction.

- Differences between builders' homes and the competition.

Evaluating the On-Site Salesperson

To properly evaluate a salesperson, they must accompany you on the model home tour. Therefore, you must communicate your visit expectations so there is no mistake about what you want to accomplish. To remind you, here is the example I provided earlier with some modifications to fit your first encounter situation:

***

My purpose for today's visit is to learn about the community and the builder, and familiarize myself with your homes. I was hoping you could walk me through the model home today and highlight what makes your home different from your competitors.

***

By communicating your visit expectations, you established your purpose. You confirmed that you want to learn about the community and the builder. You stated that you hoped the on-site salesperson would accompany you on the tour and wanted them to highlight what makes their homes different from other builders.

By declaring your purpose, you left the salesperson no choice but to accompany you on the tour. At this point, I want you to pause and wait for a response. The salesperson with the Participator personality will jump at the chance to show the model home. At the same time, the salesperson with the Administrator personality will pause and consider your request before reluctantly touring the house with you.

Remember this: on-site salespeople communicate their intent through words, actions, and deeds. The initial encounter aims to determine if the salesperson is someone you can refer to your clients. So, pay attention to everything the salesperson says and does.

SALES CENTER DISPLAYS

Because you stated your visit expectation clearly, the on-site salesperson may begin the model home tour by utilizing one of the sales center's most important displays: the community or plat map.

A civil engineer typically draws this map when the development is first created. It is drawn to scale and shows the boundary locations and nearby streets for context.

The term plat is sometimes used when referring to the community map and is confused with plot. A plot is a piece of land used for a single purpose. A good way to clarify this is that a plat shows the collection of plots (homesites) that comprise an entire community.

Each homesite is numbered for reference, and the map is color-coded. This allows you to quickly see what homesites have been sold, what homesites are available, and what homesites include an inventory home available for purchase and possibly a quick move-in opportunity. In addition, builders will mark the homesites they consider premium with a dot or some other symbol, and your client will pay extra if they choose that one.

The community or plat map is updated as sales occur and inventory homes are added. Thus, it is an excellent place to learn about current sales and inventory home construction status, and availability.

When the salesperson directs you to the community display before entering the model home, this is a sign that the salesperson is adhering to their training by introducing a client to the community before touring the model home. It also opens up an opportunity for dialogue, including questions about things the salesperson needs to know. It also allows clients to ask questions to learn valuable information about the builder and the community. In other words, it is a win-win for the client and the salesperson.

How to Participate in the Community Map

You should expect the salesperson to provide an overview of the community. It includes the following:

- The number of homes to be built in the community.

- Houses sold to date.

- Number of house designs available in the community (single-family, multi-family, zero lot line, semi-custom, and custom).

- Number of inventory homes available for sale.

- Age of the inventory homes.

- Plans for any future development.

You should also expect the salesperson to ask questions about your current housing situation and your intent to purchase. When asked a question, answer it using the backstory you created.

The Community Map

What follows is a typical dialogue the salesperson might use to introduce the community using the community map, and how you can use their words to transition to things you need to know about the community.

Salesperson: *Before we tour the model home, I'd like to introduce you to our community. Would that be okay?*

You: *Sure, I have driven through the community and have some questions for you.*

Salesperson: *This is our community map. For reference, the homesites with yellow houses are available for sale, the red houses are sold, and the green-colored houses are inventory homes. Do you have a time frame for moving into your new home?*

You: *That depends. We have a house to sell, but we are confident it will sell quickly. You mentioned inventory homes. I see there are five of those. Are they complete and ready to move into?*

Salesperson: *Two of our five inventory homes are complete; two are in various stages of construction, and one just started. I believe the foundation was poured last week. It sounds like you might be interested in one of our inventory homes. Please share with me what you want in a new home.*

You: *Well, no final decisions have been made yet, but we know we want four bedrooms, a larger family room than we have now, and, if possible, separate closets in our bedroom. Do either of the finished inventory homes have what we are looking for?*

Salesperson: *The two completed homes have four bedrooms and large family rooms. Two of the ones under construction have four bedrooms, and the other, I believe, only has three with a bonus space that can be converted into a bedroom, but right now, it is set up as an office space.*

You: *After touring the model home, can we look at several of your finished inventory homes?*

Because you knew what to listen for, it was easy to transition from the salesperson's descriptions of the community's sold, available, and inventory homes. Following the model home tour, you also confirmed a visit to several of the inventory homes.

Selling is easy if you know what information your clients require to make an informed decision. In every sales presentation, the salesperson will ask qualifying (what is important to them) and discovery (what is important to you) questions, allowing you to follow up with your need-to-know questions. The answers you receive will help you determine whether the community, the builder, and the salesperson are right for you and your clients.

In Book Three of this series, *Have You Considered the Possibility of New,* I will provide a roadmap to discover what is important to your clients. With this information, you can review the profiles of your builder partners and choose the one that best provides your clients with a home that fits their needs and wants.

Transitional Listening

Before moving to the model home tour, I want to emphasize a skill that will set you apart from every on-site salesperson and your peers. That skill is transitional listening. I am sure you are familiar with the terms active and passive listening. If not, active listening involves fully engaging with a speaker by actively participating in the conversation, providing feedback, and showing understanding through nonverbal cues such as nodding. In contrast, passive listening means simply hearing the words without actively responding or processing the information, often indicating a lack of full engagement with the speaker.

The difference between active, passive, and transitional listening is that transitional listening enables you to transition smoothly by paying attention to the trigger words the salesperson uses. In the previous dialogue, the salesperson introduced you to the community map by identifying available, sold, and inventory homes. The word *"inventory home"* triggers you to transition into the information you need about the builder's inventory home strategy.

The sales presentation becomes a conversation between you and the salesperson, where you learn something important. The key to transitional listening is knowing what words to listen for. I reviewed these earlier, but here they are as a reminder:

- Builder

- Builder policies and procedures

- Location

- Community

- Homes and options

- Homesites

- Financing

- Competition

- Pricing

So, you can follow up with your question whenever you hear one of these trigger words during a sales presentation. The best way to get the salesperson to provide information that is important to you is to use one of the following bridge phrases somewhere in your follow-up question:

- I was wondering ...

- I am curious ...

- I'd like to know ...

- Would you mind sharing ...

- I am glad you mentioned it ...

What follows are some examples that demonstrate how to move from a trigger word you heard using a transition phrase:

- "*You mentioned earlier* that you have a list of *preferred lenders. I'd like to know* what types of financial programs they offer.

- "Earlier, you said something about earnest money. *Would you mind sharing* with me how much *earnest money* you require?"

- Earlier, we were discussing the *community. I am curious:* how many homes have you *sold to date*?"

- "You mentioned the *location* and its convenience to several lakes. My husband and son both enjoy fishing. *I was wondering* how close those lakes are.

- "Before we proceed, you mentioned accepting contingent contracts." *I'm glad you mentioned it,* because we have a house to sell. What *is your contingent contract policy?*

I underlined the trigger word, the transition phrase, and the information you wanted to secure in these examples. It is easy to see that when you know what to listen for and how to use transition phrases, the sales presentation becomes a conversation with two or more people working toward a similar goal: selling and purchasing a new home.

Client Registration Card

After the community map review, one last thing likely to occur is being asked to complete a registration card. A new home builder's client registration card typically includes the client's contact information, whether a real estate agent represents them, and how they were introduced to the development. What follows is a more detailed breakdown

- **Contact information:** This includes the client's name, phone number, email address, and physical address.

- **Representation**: The registration card typically asks whether a real estate agent represents the client and, if so, identifies the agent by name.

- **Source of lead**: The card may ask how the client learned about the community (e.g., online, from a real estate agent, through a social media ad, etc.).

- **Additional information**: Most volume builder registration cards ask about the type of home the customer is interested in, their budget, and their timeline for purchasing, which may also be included.

When asked to complete the registration card, please do so thoroughly. Do not leave any questions unanswered. Provide your phone number and non-real estate email address. One of the most critical evaluations you will make about the on-site salesperson is their willingness to follow up.

Model Home Tour

You have toured the community and feel confident you could refer it. You have walked through homes under construction and may have also walked through an inventory home on your own or with a construction supervisor. Like the community, you can confidently refer the builder and the quality of their homes to any of your future new home clients.

The model home tour is the last step in your evaluation process. It may be the most crucial because, for the first time, you will hear from the on-site salesperson an explanation of the home's standard features, available options, structural upgrades, and what sets the builder apart from its competitors.

To accomplish all of the above, you will want to do the following:

- Allow the on-site salesperson to present the home without interruption.

- If asked questions throughout the model home demonstration, answer them and follow up with a discovery question about the community or builder. Remember, your goal is to have a conversation that benefits you and the salesperson.

- If you have not completed a registration card and are asked for your contact information, provide it.

- Ask permission to take pictures and notes.

- Respond if the on-site salesperson follows up with you via email, text, or phone.

Below is a brief explanation of what to expect from the on-site salesperson during the model home tour.

Model Home Presentation

Before I explain what to expect during the model home presentation, I would like to clarify the typical actions of a new home buyer as they tour the model home for the first time. I offer this information because, as a secret shopper, you will want to mimic their behavior. They want to:

- Look.

- Compare.

- Contrast.

- Ask questions.

- Eliminate.

After reading an explanation of each step, pause for a moment and reflect on your most recent purchase. That purchase may have occurred on your way to your real estate office today. You may have stopped to purchase a soft drink and a sandwich. Before making that buying decision, you had to _look_ at the items on the menu. You _compared_ one item against another, then _contrasted_ it against what you may have had for lunch yesterday. If you watch calories, you _compare_ the soft drinks and decide whether to order a diet soft drink or a regular soda. Finally, you *eliminate* the chicken sandwich and regular soda and purchase the hamburger and diet soda.

What I described is what I refer to as a purchasing process. This behavior of looking, comparing, contrasting, questioning, and eliminating occurs whenever you make a purchasing decision. To be a believable secret shopper, follow your buying behavior. The following is a brief explanation of each step in the purchasing process as it relates to home buying:

Home Buying Process

Look

In his book *Raving Fans,* Ken Blanchard writes that a customer's initial focus is narrow. He states that a customer's first desire is to experience the product before interacting with the salesperson. Once the customer decides the product looks and feels right, Blanchard believes a salesperson earns the right to ask discovery and qualifying questions and share the product's value. He reasons that until the customer has experienced the product, they feel unqualified to respond to a salesperson's questions.

This scenario is acted out whenever someone visits an open house. Take a moment to reflect on your last open house. Did the people want to engage with you before looking, or did they want to avoid you? Based on my years of experience, I know the answer is to avoid. They want to look at and experience the house before answering questions and listening to your sales presentation. So, as a secret shopper, follow in the footsteps of your clients as you walk through the model home and do what they do—look.

Compare

Comparing is the most crucial step in a home buyer's purchasing process. During this step, they assess their feelings about what they are experiencing. If the home feels right, they want to know more about it. If what they are seeing and experiencing doesn't compare to what they have in mind, they are ready to move on to the next experience.

Remember what I wrote: *"Move on to the next experience."* I didn't say move to the next community. There is a difference between a new house experience and a new community experience. Every new house tour offers a unique and distinct experience. The more homes a buyer tours, the more experience they have to compare. The builder you have chosen may provide several models and inventory homes to view. I want you to tour everything the builder offers, because each model or inventory home provides a unique encounter.

As a secret shopper, I want you to keep in mind that as you tour a model or inventory home that what you are seeing is a representation of three things:

1. Quality of construction.

2. Standard features.

3. Personalization.

As you review, please compare the quality of construction to that of other model homes you have toured, the list of standard features to those of other homes you have experienced, and, lastly, the options you see in other homes you have viewed. If you notice something that separates this builder, take a picture to include in your Digital Builder Binder.

Contrast

Webster's online dictionary defines contrast as *"to appraise concerning differences."* This definition outlines the expectations for you as you tour the model home. Please look for the differences the model home offers compared to other experiences you may have had with homes from different builders or resale homes. The contrast you see sets one builder and house apart from another. The contrast may be positive or negative, but it represents the type of information you will want to share with your clients. The contrast may be the thing that either eliminates the house or causes the house to make your client's shortlist.

Question

As you examine the model home and compare it with your mental image, I want you to ask questions about what you are experiencing. Your questions let the salesperson know you are a serious home buyer. When the on-site salesperson senses your interest in the home, they will provide you with additional information. Your questions aim to learn more about the builder's products and their benefits, and evaluate the salesperson's knowledge of the products they are selling.

The questioning step in the home-buying process is essential because the answers you receive determine whether you eliminate the house you are considering and move toward another that may provide the experience you and your clients are looking for.

Eliminate

The elimination step is the easiest to understand and relate to. Think about it. When you go out to make a purchase, are you there to buy or to eliminate? Most likely, your answer is to eliminate.

To make my point, let's examine what happens when you go out to purchase a shirt or blouse. As you wander through the rows of shirts and blouses, you pick one up, look at it, compare and contrast it against what you have in mind, and then eliminate it because it just doesn't look or feel right. This purchasing decision pattern is repeated in every purchase we make. Look, compare, contrast, ask questions for clarification, and eliminate if it is not what you had in mind. It is that simple.

As a real estate agent, you will experience a lot of elimination. Therefore, you must be okay with the idea of elimination because you are not being eliminated; instead, it's the house, the homesite, the community, the location, the financing program, or the builder being eliminated. Elimination is not something to be taken personally. Your role as a real estate professional is to provide your clients with solutions to their housing needs. What is being eliminated is the solution you are providing.

The great thing about what I just explained is that you can incorporate the purchasing decision process into your sales presentation for new and resale alike. All you have to do before your client enters the home is say the following:

***

When you enter the house, I want you to take a moment to <u>look</u> around and <u>compare and contrast</u> what you see with what you have in mind. I'll be here to answer any <u>questions</u> you may have. If what you see is not what you had in mind, we will <u>eliminate</u> it and proceed to the next home and community on our list. How does that sound?

***

I promise you this will work every time with every buyer, whether your client is considering a new or resale home. It will work because you give your client permission to do as they wish. They want to look before answering questions; they want to compare what they see to what they have in mind; they want to contrast differences from what they currently have; they want answers to their questions, and finally, they want it to be okay to eliminate and move on.

It's showtime: the model home tour.

Model Home Tour Expectations

Sales managers and trainers instruct on-site salespeople on demonstrating the model home. They focus their training on seven areas that, if done correctly, position the house and the builder as something and someone that will meet and possibly exceed their new home expectations related to design, products, and quality. Those seven areas are:

- To establish the on-site salesperson's credibility through product knowledge.

- To sell the builder and their reputation for quality construction.

- To explain included standard features, options, and structural upgrades.

- To ask any remaining discovery and qualifying questions.

- To guide potential home buyers in making minor decisions by utilizing tie-down and trial-close questions.

- To sell a trip to a homesite, where clients can experience where their future home will be built.

- To tour the community so the client can see what has been built, to offer a tour of a home under construction, and possibly experience a completed inventory home.

If you are an experienced Realtor, I am sure you will look at the list above and smile because you have never experienced anything like what is described. While that may be true, I want you to be prepared for a professional on-site salesperson capable of executing the above. Additionally, remember your role as a secret shopper is to evaluate the selling skills of the on-site salesperson.

The following bullet points revisit key points that were discussed before. Although these suggestions have been covered, they do merit repetition for clarity and emphasis.

- Allow the on-site salesperson to present the home's features and benefits uninterrupted.

- If asked questions about your current situation, answer them.

- If asked to tour the community, look at available homesites, walk through an inventory or under-construction home, I would like you to do so.

- Take photos, but ask for permission first.

- Take notes.

- If followed up by the on-site salesperson, respond promptly.

What follows is a description of how you are to evaluate the salesperson using the above suggestions.

Features and Benefits

On-site salespeople have been taught the value of selling new home product benefits for years. Books have been written on the importance of presenting product features and connecting them to the benefits. If you asked the on-site salesperson, they would admit that selling product benefits is at the core of a successful model home sales presentation. Yet the fact remains that most on-site salespeople do not sell product benefits to any significant degree. Why? The reason is based on two faulty assumptions that most builder salespeople make about new home buying prospects: the first assumption is partially correct and the second assumption is entirely incorrect. Here is an examination of both assumptions:

- **First assumption**: New home prospects are aware of product benefits. While this may be true of some products, it is not universally true.

- **Second assumption**: The on-site salesperson assumes the prospective home buyer is considering product benefits.

Both of these assumptions can lessen the impact of the on-site salesperson's sales presentation. Unless a new home buyer considers the benefits during the sales presentation, there is no way they will adequately value the products that a builder includes in the home. Therefore, it cannot be distinguished unless they recognize the value of the builder's product compared to the competition. Without this critical definition, the on-site salesperson leaves the outcome of the sale to chance.

As I stated, your evaluation begins by allowing the on-site salesperson to present the home's features and benefits uninterrupted. However, for this to occur, you must know what to look and listen for. What follows is usually how the on-site salesperson has been taught to build value in the products the builder has included in the home. There are six steps to the building value process. They are:

- Discover prospective home buyers' needs, wants, and what is important to them.

- State a feature representing a single observable characteristic of the product that is meaningful to the prospect.

- Build a bridge by linking the product feature to the benefit. Some examples include:

  - This will mean to you ...

  - This will enable you to ...

  - This gives you the ability to ...

  - This will be a benefit to you because ...

- State a benefit that the product feature provides.

- Link the feature, bridge, and benefit to a buying motivation. A buying motivation may be driven by factors such as:

  - Family.

  - Convenience.

- ○ Investment.

- ○ Prestige.

- ○ Or a combination of any of the above.

- Gain an agreement through a tie-down question by establishing a value consideration in the buyer's mind. Some examples include:

  - ○ How does that sound?

  - ○ How does that make you feel?

  - ○ How does that look to you?

Here is an example of how the building value process works. The underlined words identify a step in the process.

***

Here at (builder's name), we include <u>rear-yard security lights</u> (product feature) mounted under the roof overhang. <u>What this means to you</u> (bridge) is added <u>safety and security</u> (product benefit). With both of you traveling on business overnight, I am sure you will appreciate the added security the additional lighting provides the family (buying motivation). <u>How does that sound to you</u> (tie down)?

***

The products a builder includes in the home add no value to your client unless they are brought to their attention. Making your clients aware of product features and benefits is integral to the model home sales presentation. As you tour the model home, listen carefully to see if the salesperson highlights the house's standard features and whether they link them to specific benefits. If they do, you can start to feel comfortable that you are in the presence of a skilled new home salesperson. If not, you are likely witnessing a salesperson who is just a tour guide, and someone you may want to avoid.

Discovery Questions

When the on-site salesperson asks you questions, you provide valuable information that helps them understand what is important to you. However, to be a successful secret shopper, you must understand the distinction between a discovery and a qualifying question, as you will be asked to answer both types of questions during your tour of the model home. Those questions will not present a problem because you have already created a backstory that includes answers to discovery and qualifying questions. To understand the difference between the two types of questions, the following explains each.

A discovery question is an open-ended question that stimulates thought and encourages continued conversation. They can be recognized by the following:

- They cannot be answered by a simple yes or no.

- They do not lead a prospective homebuyer in a specific direction.

- They improve dialogue by improving responses.

- They help the prospective homebuyer discover things that are important to them.

- They are used to encourage the prospective homebuyer to think.

- They provide answers to a prospective homebuyer's key decision-making conditions.

For a new home prospect to make a purchase decision, they must make six key decisions: they must decide on the home, the homesite the house will be placed upon, the location of the community as it relates to services the prospect deems necessary, the community and its amenities, how the home will be financed, and if the prospect is considering a new home, the builder.

Your role as the secret shopper is to listen for questions about the home, the homesite, the community, the location, financing, and the builder. The on-site salesperson may ask simple questions: *"What is important to you about the home?"* You are prepared to answer that question because you have developed a backstory that includes what you want in a new home.

The example I provided included what you required: four bedrooms, a larger family room, separate closets in your bedroom, and a three-car garage if you could afford it. Because there are six key decision-making conditions, you must have an answer to what you want in a home, homesite, community, location, financing, and builder.

To ensure you have an answer to any of the six discovery questions, I would like you to open a Word document on your computer and, at the top of the page, write the following six times: *What is important to me about the* ______ *?* Then I want you to type home, homesite, community, location, financing, and builder in the blank. Under each heading, please write what is important to you about each. Just write what comes to mind. I am not looking for a long list of wants and needs. Just a couple of essential things are enough.

Then, suppose the on-site salesperson asks you discovery questions about any of the six key decision-making conditions. In that case, you will have an answer, and more importantly, you can feel confident you are in the presence of a skilled new home salesperson. If you are not asked discovery questions, you are likely dealing with a salesperson who is administering the position of a new home salesperson, and someone you may want to steer clear of.

Qualifying Questions

A qualifying question differs from a discovery question in that it extracts personal information about the homebuyer that the salesperson needs to know. It also precludes any further discussion. They can be recognized by the following:

- They can be answered by a simple yes or no.

- They extract specific facts about a prospect's personal living situation.

- They help gain agreements.

- They help gain feedback during conversation between the salesperson and the homebuyer.

- They can be used to direct the conversation specifically.

- They can be used to get affirmative answers to agreements.

In Chapter Ten, I provided a list of all the personal things the on-site salesperson needs to know about a prospective homebuyer. As a reminder, here is that list:

- **Visit motivation**: The reasons a prospective home buyer visits a model home.

- **Where they are presently living**: The location of their current residence.

- **Their living situation**: Are they single, married, or have a partner? Do they have children?

- **Own or rent**: Do they own a home or rent? If they rent, how many months remain on the lease?

- **Employment**: Where are they currently working and for how long?

- **Timing and urgency**: What is their time frame for purchasing and moving?

- **Shopping experience**: Are they considering other housing alternatives (e.g., resale, renting, staying put, or another new home builder)?

- **Price range**: How much house can they afford?

- **Income**: The amount of income available to satisfy monthly mortgage payments.

- **Initial investment or earnest money**: The money they currently have available to secure the house until the mortgage is approved.

- **<u>Debt</u>**: The percentage of their monthly income assigned to current monthly obligations.

As a secret shopper, your role during the model home presentation is to listen for qualifying questions and be prepared to answer them. To ensure you have answers to the eleven need-to-know qualifying questions, I would like you to open a Word document on your computer and list each qualifying category, starting with visit motivation and proceeding through the list, ending with debt. Under each category, please provide your response to the question. Here are some examples to get you started:

- **<u>Visit motivation</u>**: Seeking a home with four bedrooms, a spacious family room, separate closets in the owner's suite, and, if affordable, a three-car garage.

- **<u>Present living situation</u>**: Currently own a single-family detached home.

The more information you can provide, the more believable you are as a secret shopper. As you answer questions, keep this thought in mind: your purpose as a secret shopper is to evaluate the on-site salesperson to determine if they are someone I can refer, without reservation, to my clients. I know no other way to assess this unless you experience the on-site salesperson's selling skills first-hand. What you experience is what your clients will experience, and I know you want the best for them.

Critical Model Home Question

During the model home tour, I want you to ask at least one critical question and several follow-up questions: *"**How much is the model home, as is**?"* Listen carefully to the answer because house base prices change frequently, and so does the cost of upgrades. So, the price you hear will be an approximation. And that is okay and to be expected.

Once you hear the price, ask the salesperson, during the tour, to identify everything that is an upgrade and its cost. Additionally, ask the salesperson what the frequency of price changes is for their houses and upgrades. My reason for these questions is that when you tour with a future client, you can point out what is standard and included in the base price and what is optional, and be able to provide an approximate cost for the upgrade, with a note that prices change frequently with little or no notice.

Be sure to include the cost of options in your notes along with photographs. You will want to add those to your digital builder binder.

Tie-Down Questions

New home salespeople are taught they won't make the sale unless they ask for the order. Throughout the model home tour, they are trained to lead prospects to minor decisions by asking tie-down questions. A tie-down question is any question that asks for an agreement. On-site salespeople know that the more they get a prospect to say, "*Yes,*" the harder it will be for them to say "*No*" when asked to make the final purchasing decision.

So, I want you to listen carefully for the following tie-down phrases that sound something like these expressions during the model home tour:

- Does that make sense?

- Do you agree with that?

- I am sure you can see how that would work for you, right?

- Does this help?

- Isn't it?

- Wouldn't you agree?

- Do you know what I mean?

- How does it sound?

- How does that look?

- How does that feel?

- Do you understand what I am saying?

Each tie-down phrase leads a prospect to make a minor decision. The result may be a "*Yes*" response or simply a nod, eventually leading the salesperson to ask the final closing question.

To understand this idea better, consider the use of the following tie-down phrases you may hear during the model home tour:

- "*<u>Wouldn't you agree</u> this floor plan is what you described?*"

- "*You mentioned you and your husband were interested in a home that featured four bedrooms. <u>I am remembering that correctly, right?</u>*"

- *This home features two closets in the owner's suite. <u>Is this what you</u>*

had in mind?

- *I recall you saying a three-car garage would be nice for storage if you could afford it. Well, this home features a two-and-a-half-car garage. It is not a full three-car garage, but large enough for storage. Would you agree?*

I have read Robert Cialdini's *Influence: The Psychology of Persuasion* several times. In it, he provides a half-dozen ways for salespeople to persuade. He writes that when people announce verbally that they are taking a position (yes or no), they will defend their position regardless of its accuracy. So, once a prospect decides to take a stand, that person will behave consistently with that commitment.

According to Robert Cialdini, consistency is one of the six ways people can be convinced. New home salespeople are trained to use consistency to get prospects to make minor decisions that lead to the big decision – a new home sale. So, the best and easiest way to lead a prospect to any decision is to use the *"Yes"* pattern, which is formed through tie-down questions. If you recognize a tie-down question, answer it with an agreement (a yes response) or ask a follow-up question to clarify it so you can agree.

Tie-down questions are part of the evaluation process, so the more tie-down questions you hear, the more confident you can feel that you are working with a well-trained salesperson who will work hard for you and your clients.

Trial Close Questions

Throughout the model home tour, you may hear several trial-close questions that test your purchasing mindset. A trial-close question is any question that requires a prospect to make a conditional commitment. Some examples follow:

- *"If you were to decide today, would you prefer the white or oak cabinets?"*

- *"I have shown you several homesites today. Do you prefer the one on Oaklawn Court or Twinberry Road?"*

- *"When you decide to purchase, will your front elevation be stone, brick, or a combination of both?"*

If a prospect answers these questions, they are moving toward a new home purchase. They have not said *"Yes"* to the house, but they have said *"Yes"* to a color for the cabinets, have selected a homesite, and have decided on an elevation. Each response represents a partial decision. When all the minor choices are combined, the salesperson has earned the right to request the order.

Consider my experience with a builder selling age-restricted housing in Las Vegas to demonstrate the powers of a trial-close. My role was to shadow the builder's salespeople throughout a sales presentation and then offer coaching suggestions on how they might improve. Before each presentation, I would sit with each salesperson and provide ways to improve individual effectiveness. On this occasion, my coaching focused on using trial-closes to gain conditional commitments.

When the time came to meet with a prospect, the salesperson was surprised. He had not only one prospect but four. Four ladies had stopped at the model home center after lunch to look at houses, making it clear they were *"Just looking."* The salesperson said he understood and led the ladies to the first model home. He introduced the ladies to the house and asked his first trial-close question. He said, *"How does this home compare with what you have in mind"?* The lady who seemed to be in charge smiled and said, *"We are just looking today. Can we look at some other models?"* He smiled, nodded, and led the ladies to the next model.

He trailed-closed again and was told they were *"Just looking, not buying."* He proceeded to the third house and asked another trial-close question. He said, *"I have shown you three homes. If you were to purchase today, and I know you are not, which house would you buy today?"* One of the ladies answered, *"I am not buying today, but if I were, I think I would like the second model you showed us."*

Her response surprised the salesperson. Quickly realizing that all four ladies might be prospects, he asked, *"I am curious, are you all interested in purchasing a new home?"* The answer surprised him even more. Not only were these four ladies interested, but their entire card club, eighteen people, were looking at new housing because the lease on their current homes was about to increase dramatically. Each was on a fixed income and could not afford an increase. The salesperson had stumbled onto a possible gold mine. Later, the salesperson and I discussed the situation. He agreed that his consistent asking for conditional commitments uncovered the real visit motivation.

Like tie-down questions, trial-close questions are part of the evaluation process. As you tour the model and listen to the sales presentation, listen carefully to see if the salesperson is leading you to minor decisions by using either or both tie-down and trial-close questions. Additionally, see if you can distinguish the difference between the two. If you can, you have learned a valuable lesson on the importance of asking questions that seek agreement and conditional commitments.

Homesite Visit

During the model home tour, you may be asked to leave the model home to look at homesites. A homesite visit must not be underestimated. I am positive you have heard the real estate cliché, *"Location, location, location."* This cliché has merit because every homesite's location is unique and different.

This exclusivity constitutes a powerful force. The late Rosser Reeves, who headed one of the world's largest advertising agencies, BBD&O, called this force the *"Unique Selling Proposition."* He claimed every product embodied a distinctive characteristic, an exceptional quality that made it desirable. In the case of homesites, the unique selling proposition is exclusivity. So, when the on-site salesperson suggests you look at homesites, say, *"Yes."*

A request by the on-site salesperson to look at homesites is another excellent signal that you are working with an experienced new home salesperson. Chances are good that, since this is your first engagement with the on-site salesperson, you will not be asked to walk a homesite itself. If you go with the salesperson in their car (my suggestion), you will most likely look at homesites through the car's windshield. And that is okay.

The purpose of the homesite visit allows the salesperson to share with you where the builder's homesites are located and their advantages. It also lets you ask homesite questions about factors that may affect a client's decision on which homesite to select. By understanding the following home site factors, you can help your clients make an informed decision:

- **<u>Slope and drainage</u>**: This may be the most crucial consideration since drainage design errors can be difficult and costly to rectify.

- **<u>Setback and side yard requirements</u>**: This is the distance a house sits back from the street and between houses. The goal is a minimum setback since it reduces the cost of concrete for driveways, sewer and water lines, and sod. However, staggered setbacks may be required for code or aesthetic reasons. The city or county sets the distance between houses, and the builder must abide by the side yard requirements.

- **<u>Trees</u>**: Wooded lots add to a home's curb appeal and salability, yet they pose special problems for construction. Trees can cause drainage issues if they inhibit grading. Plus, they are often difficult to save, so in the builder's mind, it is better to remove a tree than risk having it die, which leads to an unhappy homeowner.

- **<u>Fill</u>**: The location and amount required are essential to the siting decision. The more fill is needed, the more expensive the homesite is to develop, which may result in a homesite premium that is passed along to your client

- **<u>Sewer elevations</u>**: This is an obvious consideration, especially with low-side lots where sewage flow may be problematic.

If you see something related to the abovementioned factors that you don't quite understand, ask the salesperson for clarification. If you get a blank stare, file your question away and ask the construction supervisor when appropriate. Salespeople are taught construction basics, but they are not construction experts.

Community and Inventory Home Tour

Another reason to say "*Yes*" to a homesite visit is that it allows the salesperson to share the amenities and benefits of the community with you, show you houses under construction, and walk you through an inventory home. Most likely, the community and houses under construction tour will be done from the car's comfort.

Once again, if the on-site salesperson discusses the community as you drive toward homesites, shows you the area currently under construction, and follows up on your earlier agreement to visit an inventory home, both are signs you are engaged with a new home sales professional. And that is precisely what you want as a secret shopper.

Suppose the salesperson does not discuss the community or suggest an inventory home visit. In that case, it will be up to you to ask questions about the community and request a tour of an inventory home. Remember, your mission is to gather information to evaluate the abilities of the on-site salesperson. If you have to help them along the way, that is okay.

As a secret shopper, you are a new home buyer who can only decide when you have experienced the builder's homes, community, location, financing, and homesites. The more you experience, the more knowledgeable you become. Knowledge is what separates one real estate agent from another. To build a successful new home sales business, you must separate yourself from all other real estate agents your client and the builder have met.

RAPPORT BUILDING

If you have followed my recommendations and performed the many tasks I suggested, you have learned a lot about your selected builder, community, and on-site salesperson.

Here is a summary of the knowledge you have gathered:

- Compiled a list of national and local volume builders in your market area.

- Reviewed their websites.

- Found and read their online reviews.

- Selected one builder and community to tour.

- Confirmed your builder and community choice with your agent peers.

- Drove the community and reviewed, from your car, the construction quality and cleanliness of job sites.

- Walked a home under construction with or without the community construction supervisor.

- Walked an inventory home with or without the community construction supervisor.

- Took notes and photographs of homes finished and unfinished, and began a digital builder binder.

- Developed a backstory that included your model home visit expectations, the life change reason for visiting the model home, created answers to the on-site salesperson's possible discovery and qualifying questions, and defined your buying motivations, so you could successfully secret shop the on-site salesperson.

- Scheduled an appointment to meet with the on-site salesperson.

- Began the on-site salesperson evaluation by answering their discovery, qualifying, tie-down down and trial close questions.

- Allowed the on-site salesperson to demonstrate the model homes' features and benefits without interruption, paying close attention to what the benefits will mean to your future clients.

- Completed a registration card, if asked.

- Consented to a community, homesite, and an inventory home walkthrough.

You have been very busy, and now you must decide if the builder, community, and on-site salesperson you have evaluated are worthy of recommending to your clients. If what you have experienced feels right, trust your instincts and begin the process of building rapport with the on-site salesperson.

Chances are, you have already begun the process when you answered the on-site salesperson's qualifying and discovery questions, when you consented to a model and inventory home walkthrough, and a community tour. By participating with the on-site salesperson, you are building a connection that's based on mutual respect and understanding. This connection will continue to expand when you request builder printed material, schedule a follow-up appointment, and send a thank you note, text, or email.

Yes, I wrote, "*Schedule a follow-up appointment.*" If you feel this is a builder, a community, and an on-site salesperson, you would be comfortable referring to your clients, then you do need to return to the model home and introduce yourself as a Realtor interested in building your real estate business through new home sales.

When you do return, expect the salesperson to have plenty of questions for you, but the one thing you can count on is respect for the process you followed to find the right builder, the right community, and the right on-site salesperson for you and your clients. And respect leads to trust, and trust is the cornerstone of a harmonious relationship where both you and the on-site salesperson feel understood, appreciated, and respected.

Because you have completed the tasks as mentioned above, you are more prepared than most of your peers who wish to do business with a new home builder. Your professionalism will set you apart from other real estate agents the on-site salesperson meets, and which, over time, will earn you referrals from the builder and referrals from the many clients who will benefit from your new home knowledge.

CHAPTER THIRTEEN KEY TAKEAWAYS

Chapter Thirteen provides an overview of the key aspects you need to know to select the right salesperson for you and your clients. To reinforce your understanding of the material in this chapter, take a few minutes to answer the following three questions? Answering these key takeaways will strengthen your understanding of the chapter's main ideas and aid your ongoing learning about working and partnering with the new home builder community.

1. What spoke to you most about this chapter?

2. What insight in these pages made the most significant impression on you?

3. How will you take what you have learned in this chapter, and put it into action in your pursuit of new home sales?

Chapter Fourteen

Social Media and You

CONGRATULATIONS, YOU HAVE SELECTED a builder, a community, and a salesperson that you feel comfortable referring to your new home clients. The selection process was not easy; in fact, it was way more time-consuming and complex than you thought when you purchased this book, but you persevered, and you are now positioned to tell the builder's story, and more significantly, your new home builder story to friends, family, acquaintances, and future new home clients. I believe one of the best and most efficient ways to do that is through social media.

Social media platforms like Facebook, Instagram, and LinkedIn are valuable tools for you to build your brand, your network, and generate income-producing leads. Those three platforms will allow you to connect with potential clients, showcase your selected builders' communities and houses, and share new home-building industry trends.

Before going any further, I believe that it is necessary to point out that you must get permission from the builder's marketing department before you post pictures and share what you have learned about the builder, their communities, and new home designs. Once you have established a working relationship with the marketing department, securing permission to promote their homes through social media should only be a formality. Never forget that home builders need you and will go out of their way to help you sell their homes. Just be prepared to offer your social media strategy on how you are going to display the home designs, and how your posts are going to read. Additionally, I suggest you prepare a permission form that can be used as an agreement between you and the builder to display their homes on your social media platforms.

If you see the value in social media, then I want you to choose just one of the abovementioned platforms. My reason is that social media, unless you are already an expert, takes time to understand, develop, and organize. So, your aim should be to select a social media platform that you are currently familiar with or one that closely matches the target market you are attempting to reach.

Over the following pages, I will point out the advantages of each platform; your decision on which platform you choose should be based on your target client. A target client is a specific individual or group within a larger target market that you aim to attract and serve with your selected builders' houses and communities. Identifying your target client will help you refine your marketing efforts, tailor your message, and ultimately increase your engagement and conversations with clients who are ready, willing, and able to purchase a new home.

So, before we get started on the advantages of each social media platform, I have a disclaimer to make: I am not a social media expert and do not pretend to be one. My purpose with this chapter is to point you in the right direction regarding what platform to adopt based on the clients you desire to serve, and to provide you with content and messages you can share with those clients.

Let's suppose you don't have a favorite social media platform now. In that case, my recommendation is that you research thoroughly each platform mentioned above by Googling the term *"Realtors and Social Media,"* watch YouTube Social Media videos, and attend in-person or via Zoom Social Media CE classes offered by your local Realtor or State Real Estate Association.

When you follow the advice offered through online research, CE Classes, and the tips included in this chapter, your social media postings will display not only your new home expertise but also your day-to-day experiences with new home builders and clients.

Your stories about your new home triumphs and struggles with builders will be the foundation on which you develop a successful new home real estate business. And it will be your stories and encounters that lead clients who want to buy a new home to know, like, and trust you enough to pick up the phone and call you, send you a text, or email you.

SOCIAL MEDIA PLATFORMS

Ten years ago, there were only a few social media platforms, and you couldn't use them for anything other than connecting with family and friends to share photos. Today, however, there are many platforms to choose from, and the great thing about these platforms is that you can use them to build your real estate business.

The three platforms I recommend are free to use (or have minimal costs if you choose to do paid ads) and, most importantly, have an existing pool of users so that you can target what you believe to be your ideal customer.

To make the most of the knowledge you have gained through your builder, community, and on-site salesperson evaluations, I believe the following are the best social media platforms to achieve your new home sales goals as you move forward building your real estate business through new home sales.

Facebook

This popular platform is probably the best social medial network for real estate agents. There are many reasons for this, but here are the most important ones:

- It's the social media platform with the most extensive user base.

- It has built-in marketing tools that allow you to target specific demographics and neighborhoods.

- According to Hootsuite, two-thirds of Facebook users visit a local business page at least once a week. If you are not familiar with Hootsuite, it is a widely used social media management platform that assists users in managing multiple social media accounts from a single dashboard. The site allows you to schedule posts, monitor social media activity, track analytics, and engage with followers across your various platforms. Hootsuite may not be something you use immediately, but it may in the future become a valuable social media tool to extend your reach and influence.

- Through paid ads, you can increase brand awareness, gain more new home leads, and maximize your listing views.

Now that you know why Facebook is one of the best social media platforms for real estate agents, you may wonder how to maximize your marketing efforts. To help you with that, follow these tips:

- Use the dedicated Facebook Marketplace for real estate to highlight your selected builder's unsold inventory for free and attract new leads.

- Use the Facebook Live tool to gain exposure and interact with your audience by originating model and inventory home tours, and one-on-one interviews with the on-site salesperson and construction tours with the community construction supervisor.

- Use the poll feature to find out what your target audience considers essential when considering the purchase of a new home versus a resale home. Here are two examples that you might be able to poll: What are your likes and dislikes about the new home search? What products and features are you looking for in a new home, and what amenities (pool, walking paths, tennis or pickleball courts, etc.) are you looking for in a new home community?

- Publish Facebook Posts promoting your selected builder's open houses, inventory homes, new home designs, special promotions, unsold inventory homes, and testimonials from satisfied clients.

Instagram

Like Facebook, Instagram is an excellent platform for real estate agents because:

- Six out of ten people visit Instagram at least once per day, and they spend an average of fifty-three minutes engaging with the content on Instagram.

- Those people who visit Instagram want to see beautiful photos. It is the ideal platform for showcasing the photos you have taken during your evaluation of your selected builder's new home designs, their interiors and exteriors, the community, and its amenities.

- It allows you to use local targeting, carousel ads, QR codes, and hashtags to entice clients to reach out to you and learn more about your builder partners, their communities, and their amenities.

Due to its visual appeal, Instagram is the best social media platform for real estate agents to generate new leads. So, how can you use the Instagram platform to achieve your new home sales goals? Here are a few ideas:

1. Communicate your new home message through high-quality images and property photos (you have taken), and, most importantly, add an interesting caption that will encourage a possible new home client to reach out to you via a comment, a text, or email.

2. Post quality 15 to 30 second videos on your selected builder's house designs, structural upgrades, options, homesites, and community amenities to ignite someone's interest in reaching out to you through a comment, text, or email to learn more.

3. Through a targeted post (be sure to include photos), create interest in one of your selected builder's unsold inventory homes, a new community grand opening, or an introduction to a new home design.

4. Aim to become an influencer for your selected builder by sharing content and videos posted by the builder's marketing department (remember to get builder permission).

5. Promote your recent success stories by posting your client's testimonials (with their written permission) about you and the experience they had throughout the new home building process, including the purchase, mortgage, construction, closing, and after-sale service process.

LinkedIn

Perhaps you are not thinking of LinkedIn as a possible social media choice; however, before selling your selected builder homes, you need to create a connection with future clients, and LinkedIn is a great place to achieve that. Here are a few reasons why:

- According to LinkedIn, in the United States, their audience leans toward younger professionals, with a significant portion being Millennials and Gen Z. A large percentage of users fall within the 25-34 age range. Historically, people purchase their first homes in their late 20s to mid-30s.

- Being active on this platform can help followers understand your knowledge of new homes, which naturally leads them to perceive you as a credible real estate agent who can guide them through the new home sales, mortgage, construction, closing, and after-closing service process.

- It is an excellent business-to-business place to network to connect with the best builders in your targeted market area, and exchange valuable information with their sales and marketing departments.

What follows are some ways for you to use LinkedIn to network and develop relationships with volume builders and their in-house marketing departments, and people who are interested in learning more about the ins and outs of purchasing a new home.

- Engage in conversations to answer new home questions and promote your selected volume builders.

- Because it is a social media platform professionals use, it is an excellent place to showcase your sales achievements and new home knowledge to gain your followers' trust to either select you as their agent or refer you to a family member, a friend, or a close acquaintance.

- Having a LinkedIn account for your new home business helps you build credibility within the new home community and with your real estate peers. Because of the expertise you demonstrate through your posts, you can quickly become the go-to person within your office and your Real Estate Association for all things new home-related.

Social Media Strategy

You have completed your research on each social media platform and have decided that Facebook is the right platform for you. The next step is to develop a social media strategy that you can share with your selected builder's marketing department. Be as thorough as possible, including photos you have taken of houses under construction, completed homes, community amenities, and maybe even an example of a short video of an unsold inventory home, and several postings you created inviting people to reach out to you to learn more about the community, the builder and the new home designs being offered in your selected communities. You should expect some suggestions from the marketing department to improve your strategy, and those suggestions are a good sign that they are taking you seriously and want you to succeed. Additionally, because you want to build your real estate business by selling their homes, you might be surprised and be given photos and copy that have been professionally taken and written to improve your postings. And last but not least, secure a signed permission form that outlines your social media agreement between you and the builder.

GET NOTICED

As I was writing about the various Social Media Platforms that will assist you in building your new home real estate business, it occurred to me that I might be asking you to do too much. After all, to build a successful business, you will need more than one builder to refer. So, what you have learned about researching and evaluating the builder, community, and on-site salesperson needs to be repeated at least four times for volume builders, and maybe more if you want to include a multi-family, semi-custom and custom home builder as builder partners.

If you completed all the tasks I recommended to evaluate the builder, community, and on-site salesperson, you know, first-hand, how much time and effort it takes to vet a home builder thoroughly. The question you need to ask yourself is, ***"Do I have the time necessary to develop and execute an effective social media strategy to attract new home clients?"*** I believe, based on what you now know about evaluating a builder, the answer is "*No.*" Fortunately, there is an alternative that will allow you to post builder information without having to secure builder permission, and the most significant benefit to my alternative strategy is that it will get you noticed not only by possible new home clients but by a builder's marketing department.

What do I mean by getting noticed? That is a good question because getting noticed is the foundation on which my alternative social media rests. To help you understand what I mean, I am going to share with you a story I included in a book I wrote about my life experiences for my children and grandchildren.

Writing the book was the brain-child of my daughter, Robyn. She had read about a company called Storyworth, which sent its subscribers a question a week that would inspire the recipient to share stories and photos of their life events. These stories would then be formatted and put into a leather-bound book that you give as a gift to your family. So, as a Christmas gift, Robyn gave me a subscription to Storyworth.

It took a year and a half to write "*My Story*", but without a doubt, it was the most worthwhile writing I have ever done. It may be one of the best gifts I have ever received because my stories will live on for generations to come. My stories may lead one of my grandchildren, great-grandchildren, or even my great-great-grandchildren to make a better choice because of something I wrote fifty or a hundred years ago.

The following story was generated by the question, "*What Words of Wisdom Would I Like to Share?*" I hope you enjoy it because "*Getting Noticed*" is the foundation on which you will build your new home sales business. After reading my story, you will understand why it is so vital that you complete all the tasks I have recommended. When you do them, I promise, you will get noticed.

My Story

In 1972, Crest Communities hired me to sell new homes in Delhi, Ohio, a suburb of Cincinnati. The community was called Rapid Run Estates, and it was under development, so I began my new home sales career in a sales trailer.

New homes were in high demand, and sales took off like a rocket. Every day was better than the day before. Because of my sales and good customer service ratings, I was transferred to a more expensive community called Pontius Estates. Sales were even better in my new location.

To improve my understanding of selling, I began devouring new home sales books. My favorite author was Dave Stone, and his book, *New Home Sales*, became my constant companion. When I wasn't selling, I read and listened to books and self-improvement programs on tape. I didn't know it then, but I was laying the groundwork for a successful career in managing, marketing, researching, teaching, and writing about new home sales.

Bill Ryan, the owner and president of Crest Communities, and his VP of Construction would tour different communities weekly, inspecting the model home park and checking the cleanliness of the community and the homes under construction. During those tours, Bill would stop at the model home to ask about sales and customer concerns and answer any questions I might have. During one of his visits, he asked if I would consider relocating to Louisville, Kentucky, to manage sales and marketing in the company's first expansion city. I had been selling for only eighteen months, during which time I sold 143 homes. My hard work was noticed, and I was rewarded.

In 1978, Crest Communities was sold to Ryland Homes, a national volume home builder, and that sale opened up many new opportunities for promotions and relocations. I remained with Ryland Homes for twenty-three years. Over those years, I learned two valuable lessons:

- When you read, you lead.

- When you learn, you earn.

My advice is to stay open to every opportunity your job offers, and never stop reading, listening to self-improvement books and podcasts, and learning. If you do, you will get noticed.

ALTERNATIVE MEDIA STRATEGY

To implement the alternative media strategy, you must create a consistent daily routine to share content that your selected builders' marketing departments are posting to social media platforms. To be aware of this content, all that is required is that you follow them. You can find their social media platforms on their websites. Not all volume builders use the same platforms, but most will post content on Facebook, Instagram, and LinkedIn. In addition, some volume builders include a Realtor Registration Submission Form on their website. Be sure to complete the form and hit the submit button. You will receive a welcome email, and your goal of getting noticed takes a giant leap forward.

If you completed all the tasks suggested in Chapter Ten, *Finding the Right Volume Builder for You and Your Clients*, you have identified the builders you want to partner with, you have bookmarked them in a National Volume and Local Volume Builder folder you generated on your favorite search engine, and you have read their online reviews. You may have registered with several of the builders because you liked what you read, and have begun to receive emails and text messages inviting you to attend events, alerting you to special promotions, and notifying you about inventory homes that are available for immediate move-in.

Hopefully, you have also registered as an agent on New Home Source Professional. If you have, you are receiving emails, maybe more than you want, but that is okay because you control what builder and community information you delete and what you save. Oh, by the way, congratulations, you are getting noticed.

Because you followed my suggestions in Chapter Twelve, *Choosing the Right Volume Builder for You and Your Clients,* you have begun to engage with at least one builder by liking, commenting, and sharing their posts on your social media platforms. Chances are pretty good that you're beginning to get responses to the posts you have been sharing, and maybe you have received some positive comments, and possibly a new home buyer client. Congratulations, you are getting noticed.

Now, to increase your exposure to a larger homebuying and home builder audience, you need to block twenty minutes each day on your calendar to engage with one of your selected builder partners. You decide the builder and time of day that fit best with your schedule. Some of you reading this are morning people, while others are night people. The time of the day doesn't really matter, but what does matter is that you are consistent, because if you miss a day, then the next day, rather than twenty minutes of a single builder's social media postings, you are now looking at forty minutes of reviewing social media posts for two builders. Finding twenty minutes in a day is doable; finding forty open minutes in a day may be difficult.

Be consistent, and your builder partners and future new home buyers will notice you.

One additional suggestion is that you have dedicated social media platforms for your real estate business. It is not recommended that you combine your family social media platforms with your business platforms. Your family and friends want to see pictures of your children, the wedding you attended over the weekend, and the new restaurant you tried last night, but people who are following you because of your new home expertise won't care about your personal life (until they get to know you). So, create social media platforms that focus on new home builder content only. When you do that, you will get noticed.

To Do List

What follows is a list of things you can do to get noticed by new home buyers and home builders. I promise that if you do the things on this list, and you take the time and are consistent with sharing your selected builder's social media postings, you will be rewarded with new home sales. Some of those sales will come from people who follow your social media postings, and some will come from builders who want to reward you by allowing you to list one or more of their unsold inventory homes or lots.

- Open a real estate business account on Facebook, Instagram, and LinkedIn.

- Open an account, if available, on each one of your selected builders' websites.

- Register as a real estate agent on New Home Source Professional.

- Block twenty minutes per day to review one of your selected builder's social media postings. Be consistent!

- Like, tag, save, embed, post, and comment on social media posts you want to share on your platforms.

- Send a message to the builder if you want to learn more about a social media post you commented on.

- Share your phone number and email address with your selected builder's on-site agent, and on-line agent.

- Attend any event your selected builder sponsors, even if the event is not in an area where you farm.

- Following a client visit to one of your selected builder partners, send the onsite salesperson a personalized thank you and include a gift card to Starbucks, McDonald's, Wendy's, etc.

- Following the close of one of your selected builder's homes, send a token of your appreciation to the onsite salesperson and the community construction manager. Be sure you send it to the builder's office, not the model home. The reason: by sending it to the office, you get noticed by all the builders' salespeople.

- Arrange a community and model home tour with your selected builder's onsite salesperson and your brokerage.

SOCIAL MEDIA RULES

I am a licensed real estate agent in the State of Texas. The following information, taken from an article written by Christine Anderson, dated September 9, 2018, is about what I need to know to comply with the Texas Real Estate Association (TREC) social media rules. I offer this information with the understanding that your State's social media requirements may be similar in some regards but different in other ways. Therefore, my purpose is to make you aware that, in all likelihood, there are social media rules you must follow before you start promoting one of your selected builders, their communities, and their homes. So, please take some time to review what you must do to comply with your State's Real Estate Association social media rules.

TREC Rule 535.155, Advertisements: For an advertisement on social media or by text, the information required (license holder's or team name and broker's name in at least half the size of the largest contact information) may be located on a separate page or the account user profile page of the license holder or team, if the separate page or account user profile is:

- Readily accessible by a direct link from the social media or text advertisement.

- Readily noticeable on the separate page or in the account user profile.

For additional information or to clarify TREC Rule 535.155, you can watch a one-hour video titled Social Media and Advertising. The video is posted on YouTube; here is the address: .

You should also speak to your broker to ensure you are complying with Social Media Rules and Advertising. If you choose this path, I suggest you have your plan available on how you intend to share Builder social media posts to your social media accounts.

CHAPTER FOURTEEN KEY TAKEAWAYS

Chapter Fourteen provides an overview of the key aspects on how to promote yourself and secure new home buyer clients through social media. To reinforce your understanding of the material in this chapter, take a few minutes to answer the following three questions? Answering these key takeaways will strengthen your understanding of the chapter's main ideas and aid your ongoing learning about working and partnering with the new home builder community.

1.   What spoke to you most about this chapter?

2.   What insight in these pages made the most significant impression on you?

3.   How will you take what you have learned in this chapter, and put it into action in your pursuit of new home sales?

Your New Home Builder Story

T HE NAME OF THIS book is *Building Partnerships: A Realtor's Step-by-Step Guide to New Home Sales Success*. Its purpose is to lead you through all the tasks that need to be done so you fully understand the builder, the community, and the on-site salesperson you are referring.

For some of you, it was a journey interrupted by days or maybe several weeks when you were not reading but were completing tasks. With each task you concluded, you learned a little bit more about your selected new home builder—information you could share with your future new home buyer clients. In contrast, others have read the book from the first chapter forward, never stopping to actually experience everything necessary to understand the benefits of the builder they wish to refer. Their purpose was to understand whether what they read had enough valuable new home builder information to add new home sales to their real estate business strategy. If it did, chances are pretty high, they will reread the book, taking their time to complete the tasks.

Their journey will be longer, but both of you will end up in the same place. By completing the tasks, you will each have a story to tell your families, your friends, and your acquaintances about the benefits of buying a new home versus a resale home.

Your story will be the foundation on which you build your new home sales business. Each new builder you do business with will strengthen and broaden your understanding of new home construction, thereby increasing the credibility of your story.

But this amazing story of new home knowledge will go untold unless you develop a communications strategy. To do that, I have another task for you to complete. A task, by the way, that will never end, but one that will provide the means for your new home builder story to be told, and for you to be recognized by all those you communicate with as a new home real estate expert.

THE POWER OF WHO

YOUR NEXT TASK is to read a book. As I wrote those words, in my mind I heard an imaginary loud and pronounced groan from my readers. No worries, this book is not difficult; in fact, I would categorize it as an easy read. I am confident you will find it informative and an excellent guide on how to communicate your story to the people who like and respect you, and more importantly, want you to succeed.

The book, *The Power of Who*, is only 172 pages in length. A 3 to 4 hour read at most; very doable when you break it into 30 or 40 minute reading periods.

It is available through Amazon for $20, and if you don't mind buying used, you could purchase it for $15 or less. If you want the Cliff Notes version of the book, I found a free summary PDF download. https://www.bookey.app/book/the-power-of-who. I have read it and found it to be an acceptable alternative to purchasing the book.

Bob Beaudine authored the book. He is the president and CEO of Eastman & Beaudine and is recognized as the top sports and entertainment search executive in the United States. In the book, Bob Beaudine takes the traditional networking concept, shakes it up, and rebuilds it, explaining that individuals already know everyone they need to know to be successful.

He shows readers that they already have a very effective communications network that includes the most important people in their lives: family, friends, and acquaintances. They are the people who care the most about them and will help them achieve their goals.

In the book, Bob Beaudin writes the following: "*You already know everyone you need to know to be successful*?" That statement caught my attention, and I hope it is the catalyst that motivates you to buy and read the book.

Think about it, is it possible you already know everyone you need to know to be successful? If that is true, then all you need to do is tell your new home builder story to people you already have a connection with. People who will welcome your email, text, or phone call. People who will share a post you have written about a community, a new home design, or a unique energy-efficient construction method. People who want you to be successful because they know you are not easily discouraged by obstacles, and they have seen you turn failures and mistakes into successes. Most importantly, they know you are self-disciplined and that you stick to whatever you are attempting to achieve. They know you don't give up and don't give in.

Bob Beaudine calls these people your "*Who*" friends. Your "*Who*" friends are not only supporters, but most likely, they are the people you turn to for advice. They are the ones who save you from negative self-talk by providing you with the encouragement to move toward your goals. It is your "*Who*" friends whom I want you to nurture. They are the ones I want you to ask for help in building your new home real estate business.

Have I caught your attention? Have I convinced you to buy the book? If not, did I at least convince you to download the PDF summary? If I have, you probably have already begun to identify your Inner circle, your "*Who*" friends, people who will become your "*Allies*", your "*Advocates*", your "*Acquaintances*", and "*Fans*". These are the people who make up your "*Who World*." You now have a list of people who you can connect with and want you to succeed, and are willing to share your new home builder story with their "*Who World*."

Now, let's look at how email and text can be the method to deliver your new home builder story to your "*Who World*."

EMAIL MARKETING

To market your new home builder story via email, you must adhere to some precise requirements, they are: segment your "*Who World*" into home buying groups, then personalize your new home content to your various home buying segments, use high-quality visuals, include a clear call to action, and most importantly, ensure your subject lines encourage opening.

Let's look at each email requirement to better understand what is necessary to write an effective email that will be welcomed, read, and shared.

Segment Your Home Buying Groups

Your *"Who World"* probably includes different home-buying groups. What follows are generational trends that most likely make up your inner circle:

- **Baby Boomers**: Baby Boomers (1946 to 1964) account for a large portion of home buyers, driven by a desire for smaller homes, closer to family and friends, and possibly due to health-related factors.

- **Millennials**: Millennials (1981 to 1996) continue to be a significant buying force, with a high percentage of first-time home buyers among younger millennials and a high percentage of married couples among older millennials.

- **Gen X**: Gen Xers (1965 to 1980) often lead in multi-generational home buying, with a significant portion of buyers in this age group purchasing homes to care for or spend time with aging parents.

- **Gen Z**: Gen Z (1997 to 2012) represents a smaller share of home buyers but has the highest percentage of single female buyers.

Now, take some time to examine your list, starting with age. Does your *"Who World"* consist of a combination of all the above, or does it favor one buying segment over the other? Let's suppose you are trending toward Millennials (26-44), followed by Baby Boomers (59+), then by Gen Xers (45-58).

For purposes of the following exercise, please focus your attention on Millennials. **YOUR TASK** is to research Millennials' home-buying characteristics. Here is what I found out by Googling "Millennial Home Buying Characteristics."

Key Characteristics:

- Smart home technology.

- Open floor plans.

- Affordability and location.

- Sustainability.

- First-time homebuyers.

- Size and features.

- Modern upgrades.

All of the above information will help you target your email message based on interests, which leads to the next email requirement: personalize content.

Use Names and Specifics

Make each email feel tailored to the recipient by using their name and addressing their specific interests. Here is an example:

***

Hi (first name), I hope this message finds you well. One of my new home builder partners is proud to offer cutting-edge smart home technology that empowers homeowners to seamlessly control appliances, thermostats, lights, and other household devices.

This innovative technology is designed to provide both convenience and significant cost savings. After experiencing the model home, I couldn't help but think that this might be something you would find intriguing. It represents a new era of living, where efficiency and comfort meet.

If you or anyone in your network is interested in learning more about these remarkable new home innovations, please don't hesitate to reach out. I am committed to working diligently for you and your referral and will ensure that all your questions are answered thoroughly. I look forward to hearing from you soon.

***

Any one of the abovementioned characteristics can be used with this email by changing out the characteristic. Here is an example using the open floor plan characteristic.

***

Hi (first name), I hope this message finds you well! One of my new home builder partners has crafted a breathtaking open floor plan that truly redefines modern living. After touring their model home, I couldn't help but think this might be something that would catch your interest, as well as [spouse or partner's name].

This thoughtfully designed space offers a seamless blend of elegance and functionality, ideal for entertaining, relaxing, or simply enjoying the beauty of a well-crafted home. I've attached a photo so you can get a glimpse of its charm.

If you or anyone you know would like to learn more about this remarkable floor plan, please don't hesitate to reach out. Feel free to share this message, and copy me so I can ensure they receive the attention they deserve. I promise to put my utmost effort into supporting you or anyone you refer, looking forward to connecting with you soon!

***

A question that comes up often in my seminars is about sending generic emails to everyone in your inner circle. My answer is, by all means, send out generic emails if the content has meaning to your whole inner circle.

However, there is one requirement that you must adhere to.

Use Blind Copy

A blind copy (BCC) in an email is a way to send a copy of your email to multiple recipients (Inner Circle) without them being able to see each other's email addresses. This helps protect the privacy of the recipients and prevents unsolicited replies from being sent to the entire list.

Here is an example of an email that can be sent to your entire inner circle using BCC.

***

Greetings! I am thrilled to share some exciting news about my professional journey. I am now redirecting my real estate expertise toward developing a new home sales business. This new focus represents a dynamic step forward in offering clients opportunities to embrace the joys and benefits of purchasing newly constructed homes—homes that are tailored to modern lifestyles.

With my real estate license and dedication to excellence, I am committed to guiding clients through every step of the process—whether it's understanding the benefits of new construction, selecting the perfect property, or navigating contracts and negotiations. If you or someone you know would like to <u>learn more</u> about the possibilities of owning a newly constructed home, please don't hesitate to reach out.

I promise to work diligently to ensure that your experience, or that of your referrals, is smooth, rewarding, and enjoyable. Your trust means everything to me, and I am here to provide the expertise, dedication, and personalized service you or they deserve. Let's make dreams a reality together! I look forward to hearing from you soon.

***

This email's purpose is to announce your aim to build a new home sales business. Because builders offer an enormous number of opportunities to reveal their activities, you have limitless material to share with your inner circle. Here are just some of the types of things you can broadcast:

- New community announcement.

- New home buying tips.

- New inventory listing available for immediate move-in.

- Open house invitation for new model home.

- Share a builder's press release.

- Share a builder's blog post.

- Share a new home design.

- Share a testimonial from a satisfied new home buyer client.

- Announcing a special builder promotion.

- Etc.

As you can see, the types of generic messaging to your inner circle are vast. You will never run out of messaging opportunities because builders are always doing something to attract people to their communities. All you have to do is be aware of what your builders are doing by following them on social media, then share their marketing message as an email announcement.

A good question you might be thinking about is: ***How often should I send out a generic message to my inner circle***? I suggest you limit generic messages to one per month. My reason is twofold:

- I don't want you to wear out your welcome. Email fatigue is a real thing. It is the feeling of frustration when you flood someone's inbox with too many emails. This can quickly lead to a request to unsubscribe. And that is not what you want from someone in your inner circle.

- In email campaigns, there is a lingering impact, which is called a residual effect. It means the impact of your email doesn't just disappear after the email is read, especially if your emails come in a consistent pattern (once a month).

Think of it like building a memory or impression in the minds of your inner circle. Those impressions continue to affect how your inner circle thinks about new home construction and the person who has influenced their thinking. Because of your consistent email announcements, that person is you! So, when someone in your inner circle is considering a move or a friend, family member, or acquaintance mentions the possibility of moving, it is your name they refer to.

The next email requirement is the use of high-quality visuals. I am sure you have heard the phrase *"A picture is worth a thousand words."* The saying means, as it relates to new home construction, an image can quickly communicate a builder partner's design feature that would take many words to describe.

The following offers some suggestions on how you might use the images you have taken while touring a new home community and the model or inventory homes.

Showcase Properties and Communities

When you deem appropriate, incorporate the high-quality photos you have taken during your research for the right builder, community, and on-site salesperson.

One of the emails I shared earlier included a photo of an open floor plan. The words I used to describe the characteristic represent a call to action to open the photo attachment. They are as follows:

***

This thoughtfully designed space offers a seamless blend of elegance and functionality, ideal for entertaining, relaxing, or simply enjoying the beauty of a well-crafted home."

***

When you combine a floor plan description with a picture, it is almost impossible for the recipient to resist the urge to open the photo to see what you attached.

To effectively use photos in emails, here are some recommendations:

- **Don't rely solely on images:** Never send an email that consists of only images. This can trigger spam filters and hinder deliverability.

- **Maintain text-to-image ratio:** Aim for a good balance of text and visuals, like an 80:20 text-to-image ratio.

- **Use alt-text:** Always include alt-text for your images. This allows recipients to understand the email's content even if images are blocked. It is also important for accessibility and helps those within your inner circle who are visually impaired.

- **Avoid putting information in images:** Don't put information or a call-to-action within images, as they might not be displayed.

- **<u>Test across your inner circle</u>**: Test your emails with several people in your inner circle to ensure the photos you have attached are rendering correctly.

By following these tips, you can effectively use visuals in your emails to make them more engaging and informative for your inner circle.

Call to Action

The next requirement for an effective email is a clear call to action (CTA). A CTA is a prompt that encourages the recipient to take action. This action could be anything from downloading content like a blog post, a photograph, a testimonial, booking a showing appointment, to learn more, or even completing a five-minute survey. You include a CTA to continue a conversation or an interaction between you and someone in your inner circle. In the email examples I shared with you, I used *"learn more"* and *"share this message"* as my CTA.

Here are the key elements of a strong CTA:

- **<u>Clarity</u>**: A good CTA should be short, typically two to five words, and clearly convey the action you want the recipient to take. Phrases like *"Learn more"*, *"Share this message"*, and *"Schedule phone meeting"* are effective because they are direct and easy to understand.

- **<u>Create urgency</u>**: Incorporate a sense of urgency to motivate quick action. Creating urgency through the marketing efforts of volume builders is easy because they are always promoting discounts, price changes, immediate move-in opportunities, lower interest rates, discounts on popular options, and grand openings of a new model home or availability of new community sections that feature larger or smaller lots that back up to a green space, or require less exterior maintenance. Use phrases like *"Limited time offer"*, *"Don't miss out"*, *"This month only"*, and *"Call me today"*.

- **<u>Make your CTA stand out visually</u>**: To make a CTA visually stand out, consider using bold or italic fonts and underlines. In my CTA examples, I provided a sample of bold, italic fonts and the use of an underline. Ask yourself, did you notice the difference? Did the CTA stand out? Did it encourage you to open the attachment? By implementing any of these strategies, you will create CTA's that are visually compelling and effectively guide your inner circle towards a desired action.

Additionally, the use of color fonts is something that will draw attention to your CTA. Different colors evoke different emotions. Red and orange create a sense of urgency, while green can imply action.

Some additional things you can do to draw attention to your CTA are to change the font and the font size. In one of my examples, I changed the font from Times Roman to Baquet Script and the font size from thirteen to fifteen. Did you notice the difference?

The point I want to make is to be creative with your call to action. Continuously test different variations to see what works best for your inner circle. You have many options; make sure you do something to make your CTA get noticed.

Now, onto your last email requirement, which may be the most critical requirement: writing compelling subject lines.

Grab Your Recipient's Attention

The subject line is the first thing your inner circle sees, so you must make it enticing to open. An email subject line is a brief text field in an email that summarizes the email's content, appearing in the recipient's inbox before they open the message. It is the first impression and greatly influences whether the recipient will open and read the email. A good subject line is clear, concise, and relevant, providing a reason for the recipient to engage with the email.

Here is a close look at the key characteristics of a good subject line:

- **Clarity**: State the main message or purpose of the email directly.

- **Conciseness**: Keep it short and to the point, ideally under 40 characters.

- **Relevance**: Ensure the subject line accurately reflects the email's content.

What follows are subject line suggestions for the three email examples I provided:

- **Smart home technology email**

  - Smart home technology, a more intelligent home life

  - Automate your life with smart home technology

  - Say hello to automated homes

- **Open floor plan email**

- ○ Elevate your lifestyle with an open floor plan design

- ○ Embrace modern living with an open floor plan design

- ○ Discover the breathtaking open floor plan now

- **Developing a new home sales business email**

  - ○ Guiding clients through the new home construction process

  - ○ Unlock the secrets of new home construction with a trusted guide

  - ○ Exploring the many benefits of new home construction

  - ○ End the guesswork in new home construction: Exclusive insights with (your name)

By following the abovementioned tips and continuously testing different approaches, you can craft a compelling subject line that increases your email open rates and improves the overall success of your emails.

TEXT MARKETING

In today's competitive new home market, staying connected with your *"Who Friends"* is critical if you want to build your real estate business. Text message marketing, unlike email marketing, offers a method to reach your inner circle instantly to announce home builder promotions, product updates, immediate move-in opportunities, price discounts, interest rate reductions, personalized messages, etc.

The reason I wrote, unlike email marketing, is that a notable thing about text messages is their surprising high open rate of ninety-eight percent, with ninety percent of messages read within the first three minutes! This immediacy grabs your inner circles attention and encourages them to respond quickly, making it an invaluable tool for time-sensitive new home builder information.

A good example is a builder's announcement of additional option incentives available this weekend only. Sometimes those incentive announcements can be for $10,000 or more. If you have a client sitting on the fence, that $10,000 announcement may be the motivation for them to move forward.

The advantages of text marketing over traditional marketing methods are clear and easy to understand for two reasons: they are cost-effective and efficient, enabling you to reach your "*Who Friends*" without a lot of overhead expenses. And, most importantly, text marketing allows for real-time communications, which fosters a sense of urgency for your friends, family, and acquaintances to act now.

How to Market New Homes with Text Messages

To effectively market new homes using text messages, focus on providing value, personalized messages, and creating clear calls to action. Does that sound familiar? Well, it should, because text messaging has the same focus as email marketing with one exception: the original text message format, SMS, has a limit of 160 characters for a single message. If a message exceeds 160 characters, it is split into smaller parts (usually 153 characters each) and sent as a sequence of messages.

This difference is what sets it apart and makes text messaging an excellent method for you to connect with your inner circle. Never forget, people like brevity; therefore, creating concise messages will get your message read quickly. Here are some examples:

Referral

Hi (Name), (Referral name), sent me your contact information. I am excited to help you find your dream home. Let's connect and talk.

Property Update

Hi (Name), new home in (neighborhood) with all the must-have designer upgrades, and available for immediate move-in. Stay tuned for photos. Let's connect.

General Inquiry

Hi (Name), I am here to help guide you through the new home process. What are you looking for in a new home? I am available at your convenience. Let's talk.

Financing

Hi, (Name), one of my new home builder partners just emailed me that they have some great financing options available. Would you like to discuss them? Call me!

Determining Interest

Hi (Name), just checking to see if you are still interested in (Community). There is a new home that just came on the market. Lots of upgrades. Call me.

With new home builders, there is always content available to send to your inner circle. Just remember to keep your messages within the 160-character limit.

What follows are six text messaging tips. If you follow these simple suggestions, rest assured you will get noticed, and when that happens, you can count on sales and new referrals.

- Always personalize your messages with the recipient's name.

- Be clear and concise, avoid builder jargon.

- Make it easy for them to respond or schedule a call.

- Include a call to action.

- Avoid sending messages too early or too late.

- Target your messages to your demographic groups: Baby Boomers, Millennials, Gen Z, and Gen X.

CHAPTER FIFTEEN KEY TAKEAWAYS

Chapter Fifteen provides an overview of the key aspects on you can tell your new home builder story through email and text messages. To reinforce your understanding of the material in this chapter, take a few minutes to answer the following three questions? Answering these key takeaways will strengthen your understanding of the chapter's main ideas and aid your ongoing learning about working and partnering with the new home builder community.

1. What spoke to you most about this chapter?

2. What insight in these pages made the most significant impression on you?

3. How will you take what you have learned in this chapter, and put it into action in your pursuit of new home sales?

Your Success Guarantee

FIRST IMPRESSIONS ARE LASTING impressions. This is true whether you are meeting one person or a group of people at the same time. I understand the importance of making a good first impression. That's why I opened my sales training seminars with a success guarantee.

Is there a better way to make a good first impression than to offer a success guarantee? Think about it for just a moment – if someone you had never met offered you a success guarantee, how would you react? Would you stop and listen, or would you discount the person and begin to move away? I bet that at the very least, you would be curious and want to know more. After all, everyone wants success, but not everyone knows how to achieve success. So by offering a success guarantee, I immediately captured my audience's attention. They wanted to hear and know more.

Achieving success is what this final chapter is all about. Have I got your attention yet? Do you want to know more, or are you somewhat skeptical? I know I would be curious and skeptical, asking myself how anyone could offer a success guarantee. I know from experience that achieving success is a personal thing. And I also know that no one can guarantee success. To achieve success, you must believe in the following: ***If it is to be, it is up to me***.

If I'm describing your thoughts, rest assured, I agree with you. I cannot guarantee success, but I can show you how to develop your own personal success guarantee. Would that be of interest to you? If you've read this far, I'm pretty sure the answer is "*Yes*."

The ideas behind the success guarantee will change your life. Never forget they are just words now; it will be the actions you take that guarantee your success.

A Simple Idea But Difficult To Do

My success guarantee is as follows: "***Be willing to do what others are not willing to do.***" How simple it sounds, but it's so difficult to do. Understand that I am asking you to separate yourself from everyone you work with and compete with. You may think there are good reasons I don't want to do this or that, and your reasons may be legitimate. But if you genuinely want to achieve success, you must find it within yourself to begin doing what others are not willing to do.

This book, *Building Partnerships,* is filled with ideas and tasks. Have you put any of those ideas into practice yet? Have you completed the tasks you were assigned? Or are you waiting for just the right time? Consider the following experience I had with a group of salespeople in Chicago. It illustrates my point perfectly.

I was retained to conduct a series of new home building seminars spread over several months. I met with the builder's sales team one day each week. In one seminar, I explained the idea of how making a phone call to a prospect immediately after they leave the model home differentiates them from their competition.

I received nods of approval from the group. However, I still had no way of knowing whether the idea would be acted upon. Following through with ideas is entirely up to the individual. Each person makes their own choice.

The following week, one salesperson pulled me aside during the first break and told me about the success she was having with the immediate phone call idea. She had put the idea into practice with every prospect who visited her community, and she was amazed at the positive results she received. Her sales had immediately improved. She said some of her prospects had actually returned her call, thanking her for thanking them. I asked for permission to share her success with the group.

Following the break, I told the group about her success with the immediate phone call idea. I asked her to provide a third-party testimonial, which she did with great enthusiasm. I then asked the group, by a show of hands, how many had put the immediate phone call idea into practice. I'm sorry to say, not one other person raised a hand. There were thirty salespeople in the group, and only one had put the idea into practice.

What can you learn from this story? Are you the one person who takes an idea from a CE class you attended and puts the idea into practice? Or are you the person who hears an idea that sounds good but never acts upon it? If you are the person who puts ideas into action, then you understand the importance of the *Success Guarantee.* Not everyone is willing to choose to separate themselves from the people with whom they work and compete. It's easier to show up at work every day and hope something good happens. It's hard work to do things that others are not willing to do.

How do you see yourself? Are you willing to go the extra step? Have you been willing to put into practice the ideas in *Building Partnerships*? What about the tasks? Have you been willing to do those? Or are you going to be the person who puts the book on the shelf to gather dust? I hope you take the ideas and tasks contained in this book and make them part of who you are as a professional real estate agent.

A Success Guarantee Example

Another experience I want to share involves my wife, Donna, and the example she sets for our family and the people with whom she interacts every single day. Donna went to work full-time when I decided to leave Ryland Homes and open up a homebuilding consulting business. Before that, she was a stay-at-home mom specializing in raising four children and managing our household. She went to work in order to provide health insurance for our family. With a new business, I needed all the financial help I could get.

She went to work part-time for a Cincinnati department store, clerking throughout the store while keeping an eye open for a position that would hold her interest. Within two weeks, she accepted a sales position with Clinique, a well-known cosmetic company. It wasn't long before her excellent work ethic resulted in her being asked to take a full-time position. Within a year, she was promoted to counter manager and soon after promoted again to account coordinator.

Ten years later, she was promoted to event coordinator, managing a staff of fifty part-time sales associates. She achieved her success because of her willingness to do what others were not. I could share a thousand stories demonstrating this willingness, but I'm going to focus on just one. I have told this story in most of my seminars because it's a perfect example of what happens when you go the extra mile.

Donna was working behind the Clinique counter when she received a phone call from a customer who had recently been helped by either Donna or another sales associate. The lady introduced herself and told my wife she had been in that day, made several purchases, and had left behind a bag of purchases from other stores. Her reason for calling was to check if any shopping bags had been found.

Donna asked her to wait on the phone while she checked. Unfortunately, nothing had been turned in. The lady thanked my wife and started to hang up. Donna asked what other stores she had visited and volunteered to retrace her footsteps and see if she could locate the missing purchases. The lady thanked my wife, but said that it would not be necessary. Donna assured her it wouldn't be a problem because her break was coming up and she could use the exercise. Reluctantly, the lady listed the stores she visited, continuing to express her willingness to come back and search the stores herself. My wife asked for her name and phone number and promised to call back within the hour.

Donna took her break and quickly located the lost bags. She called back within the hour to relay the good news. The stressed-out customer was elated, promising to come immediately to pick them up. She arrived two hours later with a brightly colored gift bag containing a freshly-baked loaf of bread and a jar of home-made preserves. With a big smile and many words of appreciation, she told Donna that no one had ever extended the type of customer service she just received. She said the gift bag was her thank you for providing excellent customer service, and said Donna had earned a lifetime customer. She even promised to tell others about her excellent customer service experience.

When my wife shared this story, I wondered if I would have been willing to do what she had done. I've asked myself many times if, after receiving the phone call, I would look around the counter, failing to find the merchandise, return to the phone, say *"I'm sorry,"* and go on about my business. Or would I have gone the extra mile to look for the lost purchases? What would you have done? Would you look for the left-behind shopping bags? I've asked thousands of seminar attendees that question – because the answer gives insight into whether or not you're willing to do what others are not.

My wife's secret to success is her **willingness to do what others are not willing to do.** She demonstrates this willingness every day with every person she meets. And so it can be with you. Every day, you are faced with the challenge to go the extra mile. You can choose to be like so many of your peers, wait for good things to happen, or you can go out and make good things happen.

The Book's Key Concepts

The pathway to building a new home real estate business is in the pages of *Building Partnerships*. To assist you in adopting the success guarantee idea, I have highlighted key concepts from each chapter to guide you on your path to success. These concepts can be found in the book's Afterword.

When you execute these strategies, you set in motion your own success guarantee. So, as this book comes to a close, you now have a choice to make – I hope you choose the direction my wife takes every day, or you can follow the road less travelled and follow the example of the twenty-nine students who chose not to apply the immediate phone call idea. Choose wisely, because your success as a real estate agent specializing in new home sales depends on your decision. Never forget that your success in business and life depends on ***your willingness to do what others are not willing to do.***

Chapter Sixteen Key Takeaways

Chapter Sixteen provides a Success Guarantee that will set you apart from every new home salesperson and real estate agent you meet. To reinforce your understanding of the material in this chapter, take a few minutes to answer the following three questions? Answering these key takeaways will strengthen your understanding of the chapter's main ideas and aid your ongoing learning about working and partnering with the new home builder community.

1.   What spoke to you most about this chapter?

2.   What insight in these pages made the most significant impression on you?

3.   How will you take what you have learned in this chapter, and put it into action in your pursuit of new home sales?

Afterword

Once again, I want to thank you for purchasing *Building Partnerships: A Realtor's Step-by-Step Guide to New Home Sales Success.* My goal moving forward is to write six additional books, all written with the purpose of helping you understand how to connect and work with the new home builder community. The content of those books will include how to introduce the value of new homes to your clients, to understand the new home construction process, to appreciate the value of green building, to best practices for negotiating with new home builders, and finally, how to read a new home construction blueprint. It is an ambitious undertaking that will take many years to complete, but one I feel compelled to write.

What follows are the key concepts by chapter. Return to these critical concepts when you are looking for direction on how best to serve your clients and the many home builders you will be partnering with.

Good luck and good new home selling!

CHAPTER ONE

MULTI-FAMILY HOME BUILDERS

The market for multi-family housing encompasses first-time renters and buyers, move-up buyers transitioning from renting to owning, buyers interested in urban living, buyers downsizing from single-family homes to smaller houses with reduced interior and exterior maintenance, and investors seeking opportunities.

Therefore, multi-family sales and leases offer you and your buyers numerous opportunities. If you want to include multi-family builders in your business plan, it is essential to conduct thorough research to understand the market. You have three sources of information: the internet, agents you currently work with, and your local home builders association.

CHAPTER TWO

CUSTOM HOME BUILDERS

When a custom home is built, your client controls the end product completely. Your client meets with a home designer to discuss their housing needs in-depth, creating a customized plan that meets their specific requirements. All options are at their disposal, and they alone are the final arbitrator. The result is a unique home that perfectly fits your client's personality. Just remember to lean on the builder's expertise to keep your client's design and construction ideas practical and on budget.

Custom home building takes time. Prepare your client for a timeline that may reach two years from start to finish. Please discuss possible delays with your client, including design selections and changes during construction, which can significantly impact the time required to design and build a custom home.

Your commission will depend on whether you are acting as the seller's agent for the builder or as the buyer's agent for the buyer. As the builder's seller's agent, your compensation will be negotiated with the builder. As a buyer's agent, your compensation will be negotiated with the buyer and included as a line item in the final budget for new home construction. In both instances, you, the builder, or you and your client will sign a written addendum to be included in the final contract.

Chapter Three

Semi-Custom Home Builders

Semi-custom homes are the "in-between" option, falling between a production home and a custom home. With a semi-custom home, your client will choose between pre-designed floor plans that a builder has already developed. Once they have selected a plan, they can customize the design with the assistance of a staff home designer or an outside architect.

The benefits of building a semi-custom home include that it is completed faster, costs less than a custom home, reduces your client's decision-making, and offers fewer surprises during the building process. The cons are that building materials and finishes will be limited, the floor plan may not be fully customizable, and the construction process will not be under your client's control.

The commission you receive from a semi-custom builder will be similar to the compensation you receive from a volume home builder. The most significant difference between semi-custom and volume builder commissions is in the architectural changes your client contracts for. Those changes are contracted separately, must be paid in full before construction commences, in most situations, and are non-refundable.

Chapter Four

Volume Home Builders

A volume home builder constructs houses using a collection of pre-designed floor plans. Their primary focus is on construction and purchasing efficiencies to deliver cost-effective housing solutions. They build dwellings of all shapes and sizes, including single-family homes, townhouses, rental properties, zero-lot-line homes, and condos. Because a volume builder has taken responsibility for planning, permitting, and organizing the house's construction, your clients will have fewer headaches regarding the building process.

Your commission is considered earned when you are deemed to be the procuring cause of the sale. To be regarded as the procuring cause, you must register as your client's agent during your first visit to the model home, via the internet, and possibly by phone. Always consult your broker to determine the proper reporting procedure related to builder commissions, bonuses, and incentives.

The reasons to include volume home builders in your real estate business strategy are their adherence to cost efficiency, purchase security, and quick building times. The reasons not to consider a volume builder include limited personalization and minimal construction involvement.

Chapter Five

CHOOSING A HOME BUILDER TYPE TO PARTNER WITH

There are four new home builder options: multi-family, custom, semi-custom, and volume. I recommend choosing a local or national volume home builder to partner with. However, selecting the right volume builder requires research and considerable time. There are eight key factors to research when making your selection. They are:

- Reputation.

- Homeowner satisfaction.

- Mortgage and title company options.

- Variety of design options.

- Quality of construction.

- Resale value.

- Communication before, during, and after the sale.

- Standard features and upgrades.

- Problem-solving during construction and after the house is closed.

Ultimately, selecting a local or national home builder often boils down to the specific benefits each offers. What follows are the potential benefits you may encounter when deciding whether to work exclusively with one builder or a combination of builders, including multi-family, custom, semi-custom, and production builders. Those potential benefits are:

- Builder and agent partnerships.

- Home design choices.

- Builder and client meetings.

- Builder services during and after closing.

Chapter Six

<u>Managing Volume Builder Partnerships</u>

A partnership is a relationship in which individuals collaborate to achieve shared objectives. It's about respecting one another, sharing power, and feeling valued as part of a team. A Realtor and builder partnership is a mindset that, if cultivated by your actions, can result in a successful experience for you, your client, and the builder.

A new home sale can be the easiest sale you will ever make, as long as you take advantage of the benefits a builder provides. Here is the list of the nine volume builder partners who work on your behalf to make a new home sale and an easy sale:

- On-site salesperson.

- Community construction manager.

- In-office sales administrator.

- Home buyer concierge.

- In-office closing administrator.

- Builder-owned or preferred mortgage company.

- Builder-owned or preferred title company.

- Builder-owned or preferred design company.

- Internet sales coordinator.

While you will interact considerably with several of your builder partners and have limited contact with others, every one of these partners is working on your behalf. They want to partner with you; my advice is to become a friend of the builder by utilizing the resources they make available to you.

Chapter Seven

Volume Builder House Designs

A volume builder is not constructing cookie-cutter houses; they are building homes that have been professionally designed by an architect or home designer, reviewed and approved by a group of your peers and prospective home buyers, and include products and finishes that will serve your client for years, such as open floor plans, energy saving windows that allow in an abundance of natural light, high ceilings, well-appointed kitchens, ample storage spaces for clothing, garages big enough to store lawns and sports equipment, and elevations that include stone, brick, stucco, and, for many builders, maintenance-free siding.

Today's modern floor plans and elevations can take months or several years to develop. The result is a house that provides everything a first-time or move-up buyer might envision and an empty nester looking to downsize.

So, when you hear the word *"Cookie-Cutter"* or see doubt in your client's eyes when you mention touring a community that includes volume builders, take a few moments to walk your clients through a builder's new home design process. You might be surprised to learn that no one has ever taken the time to explain how a builder brings new home designs to market.

CHAPTER EIGHT

VOLUME BUILDER CONSTRUCTION MEETINGS

There are four construction supervisors and homebuyer meetings. No meetings are mandatory; however, I strongly recommend that your client attend all builder meetings. Each meeting is loaded with essential new home construction information. Here is a list of the four meetings:

- Pre-Construction Meeting.

- Pre-Drywall Meeting.

- Pre-Closing Inspection.

- Pre-Closing Orientation.

Your role during the construction/supervisor meetings is up to your client. I suggest you discuss your participation before the start of construction. Ask permission to attend the Pre-Construction, Pre-Drywall, and Pre-Closing Inspection Meetings. Provide your client with the reasons why your attendance is a good idea.

CHAPTER NINE

VOLUME BUILDER SERVICES

Volume builder services may include all three of the following services; however, remember that not all volume builders offer the same services. During your visits to the model home, be sure to discuss the type of services the builder is offering their clients.

A third-party inspection of a new home can detect problems lurking below the surface before they become big problems. It provides the builder with a written report identifying the construction issues and the best action to address them effectively.

If the builder does not offer a third-party inspection, I strongly recommend that your client hire a licensed new home inspector who has earned a home inspector certification. For a few hundred dollars, your client can know that the house they paid hundreds of thousands of dollars for was quality-built.

A third-party warranty ensures that any construction defects will be repaired during the warranty period. This includes items listed under years one and two, which warrant that the home meets specific material and labor standards.

The structural part of the warranty covers the home's structural integrity and ranges from five to ten years. This part of the third-party warranty can address issues with the foundation, load-bearing walls, or other structural components.

Not all warranties come from third-party warranties. Manufacturer's warranties are separate from the Third-Party Warranty. Appliances and other major components in the home, such as HVAC systems, may come with warranties from the manufacturer. These warranties may have a more extended warranty period than the Third-Party Warranty, so all manufactured warranties must be registered with the company that produced the product.

Most volume builders have a specific service program for the first year that allows service requests. Before calling the warranty department for service, your client should review the following documents to ensure they understand who is responsible for the repair or replacement:

- Builder Contract and Addenda.

- Limited Warranty.

- Home Owners Guide.

- Manufacturers' Warranties.

When the construction supervisor completes the punch list items, the limited warranty defines what will and will not be attended to. The limited warranty includes Performance Standards that the builder adheres to. Your client must secure the limited warranty in a safe place and refer to it before contacting the builder's warranty department.

Most volume builders accept a request for service before the builder's one-year warranty expires. After completing the punch list items, your client should begin a list of construction issues they believe are the builder's responsibility to fix. Your client should submit the list in writing to the builder's warranty department.

Your client should be aware of the possibility of an emergency and have a plan to handle it promptly when it occurs. Some examples include heating and air conditioning, electricity, plumbing, and gas leaks.

Chapter Ten

RESEARCHING VOLUME BUILDERS

There are six research steps to finding the right volume builder for you and your client. Those steps include:

- Compiling a list of national and local volume builders in your market area.

- Reviewing selected builder websites.

- Find and read their online builder reviews.

- Selecting several builders and communities to tour.

- Confirm your volume builder and community choices with your agent peers.

Prospective home buyers make six critical decisions when purchasing a new home, they are:

- Home.

- Homesite.

- Community.

- Location.

- Financing.

- Builder.

What you do when selecting a community and builder is similar to what a home buyer does when they choose. Both of you have conditions that must exist before you accept the community and builder as a possibility.

What follows is a list of wants home buyers and agents expect from a builder:

- Solid financial reputation.

- Good quality reputation.

- Variety of home designs.

- Option and structural change availability.

- Third-party warranty.

- Third-party inspection.

- Builder-owned or preferred mortgage and title company.

- After-closing service program.

- Competitive pricing.

YOUR TASK is to determine which builder on your list satisfies the wants of your future homebuyers by answering the questions provided to you.

What follows is a list of features that home buyers and agents want in a new home community:

- Safety.

- Resale value.

- Community amenities.

- Variety of home designs.

- Proximity to services.

- Miscellaneous.

YOUR TASK is to determine which community to review using the list of abovementioned wants as your guide, and answering the list of questions provided to you.

YOUR LAST TASK in this chapter is to discuss and confirm your choice of builder and community with agents who assisted you in developing your list of volume builders.

CHAPTER ELEVEN

FINDING THE RIGHT COMMUNITY FOR YOU AND YOUR CLIENTS

There are three steps to confirm your community selection, they are:

1. Drive the community.

2. Look at finished and unfinished houses.

3. Trust your instincts.

You chose the community for many reasons, including safety, resale value, community amenities, a diversity of home designs, and proximity to services. Additionally, you selected the community because it felt right to you. This feeling you have is the same one that clients experience, and it is what motivates them toward or away from a community.

As a real estate agent, you play a pivotal role in finding a community you hope will feel right for your clients. However, before you decide whether to visit a community with a client, you must review the quality of the homes your selected builder has under construction, the cleanliness of the job sites, and the look and feel of the unfinished and finished homes.

Most quality-conscious subcontractors want a clean environment in which to work and will follow how others clean up after themselves. If the house is messy when they start, they will add to it when they finish. A good rule that quality-conscious builders follow is that the home must be clean and free of unused construction debris at the end of the workday and ready for tomorrow's next subcontractor.

Look and feel of unfinished and finished homes: As you drive through the community, you must review three construction phases: foundation, framing, and exterior sheathing, and examine worksites for cleanliness.

One additional examination may be the most important because it is what clients do before visiting the model home — a review of finished houses. Suppose the houses do not look like what a client has in mind. In that case, the client eliminates the community and moves toward another development (new or resale), including the type of house they seek.

As you decide whether this is the right community for you and your clients, please consider what your clients would do: look at the community through the lens of elimination. If what you see gives you a positive feeling, trust it and make the referral. If you feel negative, trust your instincts and move on to the next opportunity.

CHAPTER TWELVE

CHOOSING THE RIGHT VOLUME BUILDER FOR YOU AND YOUR CLIENTS

To make an informed choice about the builder, **YOU WERE TASKED** with walking through a house under construction and at least one finished house built for the market. The houses under construction were pre-drywall, and the inventory home was complete and ready to move into. This direct observation of what the builder is capable of forms a basis for knowledge you can communicate to your clients.

When you walk into a house under construction, you must always wear personal protective equipment (PPE), including a hard hat, safety glasses, and safety footwear. Before entering a house under construction, you were advised to stop at the construction trailer, seek permission from the community builder, and acquire PPE if necessary.

As you prepare for the pre-drywall walkthrough, you have learned that you have two options. The first scenario involves a walkthrough with the assistance of the construction supervisor, and the second scenario requires you to perform the walkthrough examination on your own.

You were asked to consider adding a note-taking app to your phone to help you remember what was discussed during the pre-drywall walkthrough. Additionally, you were instructed to take plenty of pictures to remind you of the placement of HVAC, electrical, and plumbing locations behind the drywall.

To assist your client, you learned that hiring a third-party inspector is one of the best ways to ensure a thorough Pre-Drywall Inspection. A third-party inspector offers an impartial assessment of the builder's work and ensures compliance with building codes, helping to avoid costly repairs or disputes in the future. You learned that while some builders allow independent inspections, others may include clauses limiting or outright disallowing them in the construction contract. So, you must determine whether third-party inspectors are welcome and how the builder will respond to the inspector's report.

Like the pre-drywall walkthrough, the construction supervisor can assist with an inventory home walkthrough, or you can perform it independently. In both situations, you learned that there are three things you need to know. They are:

- The options and structural changes were added to the home.

- The builder's policy on a completed home as it relates to changes or additions.

- The construction differences between competing builders in the same community.

When speaking with the construction supervisor, be patient and allow them time to answer your questions. If necessary, ask them to pull the inventory home file.

CHAPTER THIRTEEN

SELECTING THE RIGHT SALESPERSON FOR YOU AND YOUR CLIENTS

When you visit the model home sales center for the first time, be prepared to be a homebuyer, not a real estate agent. As a prospective homebuyer, you will experience what your clients should expect when interacting with the on-site salesperson. This interaction will be the final step in selecting a builder you can, without reservation, refer to your clients and a builder you can partner with.

Most volume builders believe that what you measure, you improve. Since new home salespeople work alone or partner with another salesperson, builders cannot measure their selling skills other than through a secret shopper. I advise you to become a secret shopper to learn how your clients will be treated during and after meeting with the builder's on-site salesperson.

To become a convincing secret shopper, follow these guidelines to make your mystery shop more believable:

- Develop a backstory to support your role as a secret shopper.

- Write and commit to memory your visit expectations.

- Allow the on-site salesperson to present the home with features and benefits without interruption.

- If asked questions about your current situation, answer them.

- If asked for a phone number, provide it.

- If followed up by the on-site salesperson, respond promptly.

- Take photos (ask for permission first).

- Take notes.

Throughout this book, I have referenced setting expectations. You relinquish the buying process to the builder's salesperson without setting expectations. By establishing visit expectations, you can successfully achieve the outcome you have in mind while maintaining a high level of rapport with the builder's on-site agent and positioning yourself apart from other real estate agents.

To set expectations with the on-site salesperson, you must do the following:

- Clearly and openly communicate your needs and desired outcomes.

- Identify precisely what you want to accomplish during the model home tour.

- Ensure the salesperson understands what is expected of them while being realistic and open to compromise.

When you set expectations, you create a visit roadmap for you and the on-site salesperson to follow. When the salesperson agrees with your purpose, they have acknowledged that they will help you achieve your visit goals. If the salesperson wanders away from your objectives, you can gently pull them back in your desired direction. During a model home visit, you can choose to be in control or to be controlled. When you set visit expectations, you are in charge.

Demonstrating the model home is an essential part of the salesperson's responsibilities. Your role as a secret shopper is to facilitate this process. For it to occur, I believe it is helpful to understand what the salesperson is attempting to achieve. What follows are five things the salesperson wants to make happen:

- To establish their credibility through product knowledge.

- To sell the builder's advantages and its reputation for quality construction.

- To explain the standard features included in the base price and point out options, structural changes, and designer items unavailable for purchase.

- To ask any remaining qualifying questions and, if not already done so, ask discovery questions to understand your needs, wants, and what is important to you in a new home.

- To lead you to minor decisions by utilizing tie-down and trial-close questions.

For clarity, not every salesperson you meet has the skill or desire to execute the bullet points identified above. Most of the salespeople you meet are comfortable allowing you to walk through the model home unattended; however, that will not work for your purposes. You need to understand what makes this builder different from any other builder. And that means a model home sales presentation.

The model home tour is the last step in your evaluation process. It may be the most crucial because, for the first time, you will hear from the on-site salesperson an explanation of the home's standard features, available options, structural upgrades, and what sets the builder apart from its competitors.

To accomplish all of the above, you will want to do the following:

- Allow the on-site salesperson to present the home without interruption.

- If asked questions throughout the model home demonstration, answer them and follow up with a discovery question about the community or builder. Remember, your goal is to have a conversation that benefits you and the salesperson.

- If you haven't completed a registration card and are asked for your contact information, provide it.

- Ask permission to take pictures and notes.

- Respond if the on-site salesperson follows up with you via email, text, or phone.

If you feel this is a builder, a community, and an on-site salesperson, you would be comfortable referring to your clients, then you do need to return to the model home and introduce yourself as a Realtor interested in building your real estate business through new home sales. When you do return, expect the salesperson to have plenty of questions for you, but the one thing you can count on is respect for the process you followed to find the right builder, the right community, and the right on-site salesperson for you and your clients. And respect leads to trust, and trust is the cornerstone of a harmonious relationship where both you and the on-site salesperson feel understood, appreciated, and respected.

CHAPTER FOURTEEN

SOCIAL MEDIA AND YOU

You have selected a builder, a community, and a salesperson. You are now positioned to tell the builder's story, and more significantly, your story to friends, family, acquaintances, and future new home clients.

Social media platforms like Facebook, Instagram, and LinkedIn are valuable tools for you to build your brand, your network, and generate income-producing leads. But, before that happens, I believe it is necessary to point out that you may need to get permission from the builder's marketing department before you post pictures and share what you have learned about the builder, their communities, and new home designs. I suggest you prepare a permission form that can be used as an agreement between you and the builder.

There is an alternative that will allow you to post builder information without having to secure builder permission, and the most significant benefit to my alternative strategy is that it will get you noticed not only by possible new home clients but by a builder's marketing department.

To implement the alternative media strategy, you must create a consistent daily routine to share content that your selected builders' marketing departments are posting to social media platforms. To be aware of this content, all that is required is that you follow them.

To increase your exposure to a larger homebuying and home builder audience, you need to block twenty minutes each day on your calendar to engage with one of your selected builder partners.

What follows is a list of things you can do to get noticed by new home buyers and home builders:

- Open a real estate business account on your favorite social media platform.

- Open an account, if available, on each one of your selected builders' websites.

- Register as a real estate agent on New Home Source Professional.

- Block twenty minutes per day to review one of your selected builder's social media postings.

- Like, tag, save, embed, post, and comment on social media posts you want to share on your platforms.

- Send a message to the builder if you want to learn more about a social media post you commented on.

- Share your phone number and email address with your selected builder's on-site agent.

- Attend any event your selected builder sponsors, even if the event is not in an area where you farm.

- Following a client visit to one of your selected builder partners, send the onsite salesperson a personalized thank you and include a gift card to Starbucks, McDonald's, Wendy's, etc.

- Following the close of one of your selected builder's homes, send a token of your appreciation to the onsite salesperson and the community construction manager. Be sure you send it to the builder's office, not the model home.

- Arrange a community and model home tour with your selected builder's onsite salesperson and your brokerage.

If you decide to use social media to promote your business and your selected builders, you must follow social media and advertising rules. Check with your local and state real estate associations to learn what social media rules you must comply with. You should also speak to your broker to ensure you are complying with social media rules and advertising.

CHAPTER FIFTEEN

YOUR NEW HOME BUILDER STORY

Your new home builder story is the foundation on which you will build your new home sales business. Each new builder you do business with will strengthen and broaden your understanding of new home construction, thereby increasing the credibility of your story.

But this amazing story of new home knowledge will go untold unless you develop a communications strategy. That strategy begins with reading a book, *The Power of Who*, by Bob Beaudine. The book points out that you already have a very effective communications network that includes the most important people in your life: family, friends, and acquaintances. They are the people who care the most about you and will help you achieve your goals.

Bob Beaudine calls these people your "*Who*" friends. They are the ones I want you to ask for help in building your new home real estate business.

Your "*Who*" friends are people who will become your "*Allies*", your "*Advocates*", your "*Acquaintances*", and your "*Fans*". These are the people who make up your "*Who World*," and most likely are willing to share your new home builder story with their "*Who World*."

To market your new home builder story via email, you must adhere to some precise requirements, they are: segment your "*Who World*" into home buying groups, then personalize your new home content to your various home buying segments, use high-quality visuals, include a clear call to action, and most importantly, ensure your subject lines encourage opening.

Text message marketing, unlike email marketing, offers a method to reach your inner circle instantly to announce home builder promotions, product updates, immediate move-in opportunities, price discounts, interest rate reductions, personalized messages, etc.

A notable thing about text messages is their surprising high open rate of 98%, with 90% of messages read within the first 3 minutes! This immediacy grabs your inner circle's attention and encourages them to respond quickly, making it an invaluable tool for time-sensitive new home builder information.

To effectively market new homes using text messages, focus on providing value, personalized messages, and creating clear calls to action. Does that sound familiar? Well, it should, because text messaging has the same focus as email marketing with one exception: the original text message format, SMS, has a limit of 160 characters for a single message. If a message exceeds 160 characters, it is split into smaller parts (usually 153 characters each) and sent as a sequence of messages.

CHAPTER SIXTEEN

YOUR SUCCESS GUARANTEE

The last chapter introduces the concept of a success guarantee as a method to capture attention and inspire personal real estate growth. <u>It's about you personally being willing to do what others are not willing to do.</u>

The success guarantee involves taking proactive steps by implementing new home sales ideas shared throughout this book, completing tasks to select the right builder, community, and salesperson for you and your clients, and going the extra mile to differentiate yourself from other real estate agents a new home builder comes in contact with.

The roadmap to new home sales success involves adopting the success guarantee mindset and putting into practice critical concepts from this book, "*Building Partnerships.*" My challenge to you is to put the ideas I have shared with you into your real estate business strategy rather than letting them gather dust. New home sales success in the final analysis is a choice to take action rather than hope for favorable outcomes.

A FAVOR

If you enjoyed this book, would you consider leaving an honest review on Amazon. It helps more than you realize. Thanks in advance for considering my request.

www.ingramcontent.com/pod-product-compliance
Lightning Source LLC
Chambersburg PA
CBHW051500150726
47997CB00001B/58